Storytelling with Dolls

elinor peace bailey   noreen crone-findlay

Published by

krause publications
An F&W Publications Company

700 East State Street • Iola, WI 54990-0001
715-445-2214 • 888-457-2873
www.krause.com

Please call or write for our free catalog of publications. To place an order or obtain a free catalog, please call 800-258-0929. Please use our regular business telephone 715-445-2214 for editorial comment or further information.

Special thanks to Nina McVeigh of The Sampler House in Stevens Point, Wisconsin, for the loan of the fabulous Bernina sewing machine.

Library of Congress Catalog Number 2002113137
ISBN 0-87349-572-1

Dedication

This is a long dedication, because I'm very grateful for my many blessings! I'm dedicating my half of this book, with love and gratitude, to my parents, Doris and Ray Crone, who really appreciate a vivid imagination and their "Gypsy Child"; and also to my darling husband, Jim Findlay, and our wonderful kids, Chloe and Angus. And also to my sweet mother-in-law, Grace Findlay.

Acknowledgments

Many people help to sustain and support the creation of a book. I'm really grateful for their contributions!

There's Julie Stephani, who is the Fairy Godmother of this story, and Christine Townsend, our editor extraordinaire, Bob Best, the photographer, Donna Mummery, the book designer and, of course, all the other lovely people at Krause.

Without the love and support of friends and family, books would never get written. It's especially important to have a friend who really speaks the same language. For me that friend is Ardis Johnson. Ardis really understands the power of story! I am also blessed to have a close friend who is my dear "weaving buddy," Terri Christiansen. It's amazing how much fun two loom-loving friends can have!

And, also, Sylvie Nicolas, brilliant playwright, director, poet, and dear friend.

I also have to send big hugs of love and gratitude to my favorite auntie and uncle, June and Gene Grimes, and my siblings by birth and by marriage, and definitely by love: Lesley-Ann Crone and Alan Rosenberg, Jonathan Crone and Nathalie Schiebel, Patti and Jim Heeren, Aleksa Harkness, Judy Krzesowski, and David and Norma Crone.

And many thanks, as well, to Bernat/Spinrite Yarns, Cedar Hollow Looms, Harrisville Looms, Lee Valley Tools, Dick Blick Art Supplies, and Crafter's Pick.

How Did This Book Come About?

I really treasure hearing from readers, and so I have begun writing to authors whose work I admire. I wrote Elinor a letter, telling her how much I appreciate her work. She responded by saying that she liked my book, *Soul Mate Dolls: Dollmaking as a Healing Art.*

One thing lead to another, and we decided that we ought to write a book together. Luckily, Julie Stephani at Krause Publications agreed with us! Bless her magical heart!

Elinor and I talked by e-mail and phone about the direction we wanted the project to take. Elinor ended one of her e-mails with the statement that she had thrown the beans out the window, and we should see what would come up. Well! That phrase was the catalyst that really put the juice in the jumper! The "Beanstalk" project was born.

We decided that we would each work with the story of "Jack and the Beanstalk" and design dolls that would then be used to tell the story. We each would design dolls in our own way, using techniques and materials that we loved.

I love weaving on small looms, and so I designed my version of the "Beanstalk" people and critters in a combination of weaving and wrapping.

I began by working with potholder looms, but the folks at Krause felt that I needed to create an alternative loom – just in case the readers didn't have access to potholder looms. And so I designed the "beanstalk loom," and I am just delighted with it!

Now, I just have to share a little with you about what working with Elinor is like. Elinor and I both have schedules of teaching workshops and performing (I'm a professional puppeteer as well as designer) that would choke a horse. This meant that we would have long spells when we would have little or no contact with each other. We'd each be working on the book in our own way and then would share a brief flurry of e-mails and phone calls, and then go on our merry way. (Elinor lives in California, I live in Alberta, Canada, so distance adds another level of complexity to our collaboration.)

In spite of the difficulties of distance and wild schedules, and different styles of working (I actually ended up writing four books and designing four full sets of dolls, which drove Elinor crazy), we found that in the end, Elinor and I were both very much "on the same page." We have indeed been able to meet in the middle. (And meeting in real life was wild and wonderful, too!)

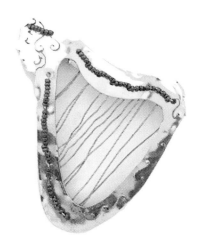

Before You Read This Book

I think that it is important to read as many versions of a story as possible when you are going to be working with it and presenting it. This will give you different perspectives from which to approach the story.

I recommend that you take a jaunt through the Folk and Fairy Tale section of your library and soak up some other renditions of the story. I've written my version of "Jack and the Beanstalk" based on the various interpretations of the story that I found. (Elinor found other variations, so her approach to the story is quite different).

It's fun to just listen to the story for the sake of the story itself, but it's also fascinating to look at the metaphors in the story. Your interpretation of the deeper layers of meaning in a story will influence the way you present that story.

Storytelling Styles

Elinor and I had a spirited discussion about our different approaches to storytelling. My style of telling stories is based on the decades of experience I have as a professional puppeteer. As a puppeteer, I strive to breathe the breath of life into the dolls or puppets. This means that I become invisible to the audience, and the characters are the focus of the audience's attention.

Hopefully, you have stories that you will want to tell in your own way. My wish is that this book inspires you to tell those stories and make dolls for them in ways that bring you the greatest of joy!

I hope that you have as much fun making these dolls and telling this story as I have had in designing them for you! See you at the Beanstalk! (And Elinor, I'll meet you in the middle of the book!)

One last note about safety – if you are planning to give these dolls to small children, please don't stitch anything to the dolls. Paint or embroider features on instead.

PS: Please don't feel that you are supposed to use these dolls just for storytelling. Feel free to make them just for the fun of it.

Noreen's Version of the Story of "Jack and the Beanstalk"

Once and twice, and perhaps not so long ago, there was a lad named Jack, who was filled with wonder at all the amazing things he saw. In fact, he was so awestruck, that he often forgot where he was going, and what he was supposed to be doing.

He and his Mother, a hard working soul, lived in terrible, grinding, gnawing poverty. They lived on the milk and cream that Mother's dear cow, Milky White, gave them. Every day, Mother pounded the churn and made butter to sell to keep the roof over their heads.

Alas, a time came when dear Milky White stopped giving milk. And so, Mother, with her heart heavy, knew that Milky White must be sold ....

Jack was convinced that he could strike a fine bargain at the market, so he pleaded with Mother to let him take the cow to the market. Mother was sure that Jack would make a mess of it, but she wanted to trust her son, so Jack set off to market with Milky White.

But then, a strange little man appeared on the road. The little man convinced Jack to trade Milky White for five magic beans that he guaranteed would grow instantly up to the sky. Jack, absolutely thrilled, agreed, because he had always longed to explore the sky. The Beanman assured him that he would meet Jack on the road again the next day, and return the cow if Jack wasn't happy with the exchange.

Jack, full of delight at his marvelous good fortune, popped one bean into his mouth, and ate it. He hurried home, to take the remaining four beans to Mother. Much to Jack's

astonishment, his mother was furious. In her outrage, she threw the magic beans out the window. Jack was sent to bed without his supper, in disgrace.

Later that night, Jack was awakened by a mysterious green light in the room. One bean had sprouted and grown, and the beanstalk climbed right up into the sky. Jack climbed the beanstalk, up, up, up and OH MY! There was the Giant's house! Driven by hunger and curiosity, he begged for food from the Giant's wife and charmed her with his pluckiness.

Suddenly, the Giant came stomping home from a night of marauding. The Giant's wife hid Jack and diverted the Giant, which saved Jack's life. Whew! Hidden though he was, Jack still heard through his chattering teeth the roaring of the Giant: "Fee fi fo fum, I smell the blood of an Englishman. Be he alive, or be he dead, I'll grind his bones to make my bread!"

After a large supper of stolen sheep, the Giant brought out three bags of gold and gloated as he counted them, but fell asleep. Jack snatched one of the bags and raced away with it. He poured the golden coins down the beanstalk and scrambled down after them.

He and Mother lived in contentment for a long time until the gold ran out. Jack decided to try his luck at the Giant's house again. So, he went to bed without any supper and fell asleep. Once again, a strange green light woke Jack up – magic afoot!

The second magic bean had sprouted. He raced up the beanstalk, straight to the Giant's house.

Once more, he charmed the Giantess, and she again saved his life by hiding him from the Giant. After a huge supper of stolen cattle, the Giant brought out a marvelous Hen that laid a glowing, golden egg. Jack, knowing that this was a treasure his Mother would cherish, waited for the Giant to go to sleep.

Sneaky Jack rushed to the hen, snatched her up, and dashed off with her. The Hen was upset at being torn away from her newly laid egg, so she made a huge ruckus. The Giant woke, and gave chase, but lucky Jack escaped.

Jack and Mother lived very well and happily from the bounty of the golden eggs.

Eventually, Jack began to wonder if there was *more* than money to be had at the Giant's house. Once again, he went to bed without his supper, and sure enough, the strange green light woke him up. A third magic bean had sprouted. Back he scampered to the Giant's house, and again tricked the Giantess. This time, she was quite wary of this naughty boy, and didn't help him at all. But, he was able to hide himself quite well because he knew the lay of the land already.

After the Giant gobbled down a huge supper of stolen

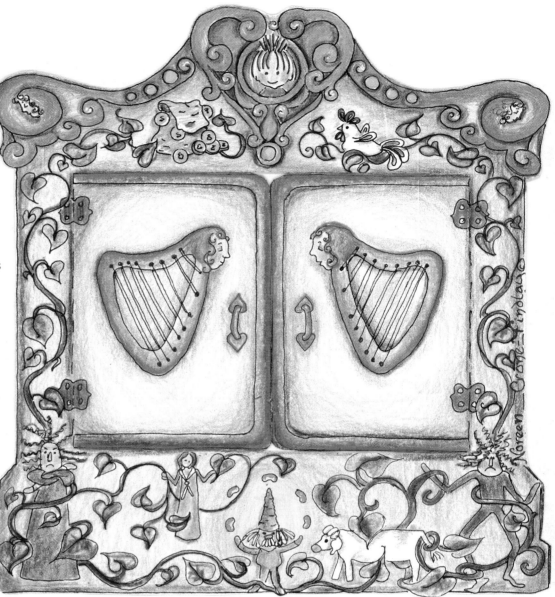

oxen, he brought out a magic Harp and snarled at her, demanding that she sing and play. The music that the Harp made was so glorious that it took Jack's breath away. Jack knew that this music was something he could not live without, so he snatched up the Harp and started running off with her.

Now, the Harp was not at all sure that this thief was going to be any better than the Giant, so she called out in alarm. The Giant woke up in a fury. He chased Jack to the beanstalk. Jack, with the Giant in hot pur-

suit, shot down the beanstalk. Quickly, frantically, he chopped the beanstalk down. The Giant fell, crashing to his death.

And so, Jack and his Mother lived long, well, and merrily – thanks to the Hen and her golden eggs. Any troubles that did spring up were sweetened, soothed, and swept away by the beauty of the harp's music.

But … the very best part is this:

The fourth magic bean has not yet grown. Who knows when or where it will? And what will grow out of it?

Interpreting "Jack and the Beanstalk"

I feel that there is a strong connection between storytelling and dollmaking. I believe that folk and fairy tales are encoded with layers of meaning and metaphor that offer insights into, and wisdom about, the way our hearts and minds work.

When we make dolls that depict the characters in a story, and then use the dolls to tell the story, we can uncover the hidden treasures of the story. We also expand our imaginations, and that helps us to see the world in a new light.

In a way, it's like playing with the elements of a dream. There is a theory that all the characters and situations in dreams are the unconscious manifestations of the dreamer. And so, we can also look at a folk tale like the beanstalk story, and see what parts of our minds and lives are reflected in it. It can help us to see ourselves in totally new ways.

The story of "Jack and the Beanstalk" is all about being filled with wonder and awe. Albert Einstein is reputed to have said that being creative means being able to look at the world in new ways, and to see new possibilities everywhere. We might say that seeing new possibilities is one of Jack's strong suits. He is awestruck by the world around him; that is key to appreciating him. He's a dreamer in awe of the wonders of the world, however, to the point of being a dawdler. This means that he's not a lot of good down on the farm. But, when it comes to spotting a wonderful and impossible thing that can lead to a whole new world, then Jack's your man.

It turns out that he's also a charming scamp and a scallywag, too. This is rather lucky for him, as he is able to charm the Giantess (who regularly cooks boys like him for her husband's supper) into saving his life.

And last, but not least, he's a person who thinks that there must be more to life than money. Off he dashes to investigate, and sure enough, discovers a Harp who sings so beautifully all who hear forget their troubles.

The key to the Mother is that she has become so care worn that she can't conceive of a world of wonders. She throws her options out the window. She fails to see the possibilities and potential in her life, and so, her life is quite joyless. She wants and needs to make a life for herself and her son, but she no longer sees a way forward. Without hope, it is impossible to believe in miracles.

And then, there is the strange little "Beanman." He is an ambassador from the world of imagination, of possibilities, of magic and wonder. He doesn't just stand at the fork in the road for Jack, he creates the fork in the road! He might be good, he might be evil – what is Jack to do? Luckily for Jack, the elfin Beanman is on the side of the angels, and not dancing to the devil's tune.

Mother would never have taken the Beanman up on his offer, and she would have missed a great adventure. Mother represents the intellectual part of us, while reckless Jack is the wild, instinctual part.

Every good story has tension in it – a pull between opposites. In this one, it is the Mother's caution that is in opposition to Jack's free spirit. The satisfying resolution in the story is that her wild, risk-taking child, fulfills all the Mother's hopes and dreams. Jack risks by going against all that makes sense to her.

In the world of story, we need a hero who is wild, free, and willing to take the leap beyond common sense.

And, ooh, those giants! Now, whenever giants appear in a story, you know that something is amiss in the kingdom. Giants don't respect boundaries, and take far more than their fair share in order to support their voracious appetites. People instinctively know this, and that's why we cheer when a little scamp like Jack puts an end to the inflated appetites of giants.

I'm so glad that the story goes beyond the physical satisfaction of bags of gold and invaluable eggs. The story ends in music. I am married to a musician; I know the healing power of music.

The Harp – the instrument that plays so beautifully that everyone who hears her forgets their troubles – represents what we should all be striving for: To create beauty, and to find the song that our soul is meant to sing. Sometimes, I forget this, so I made the Harp as a pin to wear on my lapel. When I glance in a mirror or catch a glimpse of her on my shirt, I remember to listen for the song of beauty.

Many versions of the story end with Jack ceasing to wonder so much, instead becoming a more "useful" person. That would probably be much less annoying to the pragmatic souls around him, but, really, wouldn't that be a very sad thing? I hope that we never loose our ability to wonder … that's the promise, I think, of the bean that has not yet sprouted by the story's end.

In life, there is always the possibility that something strange, wonderful, unexpected, delight-ful, and paradoxical might hap-pen any moment. Sometimes, we just have to throw our pre-con-ceived notions out the window and go to bed without our supper to make the magic happen.

General Hints and Tips for Storytelling

I am a professional puppeteer, performing for thousands of children each year. I work in the Storyteller style, which means that I am visible to the audience at all times, but become "invisi-ble" by carefully directing the audience's attention to the pup-pets. Here are some skills that I've learned over the years:

1 Rehearsing is the most impor-tant thing you can do to bring the story to life. It's the only way to discover the nuances and sub-tleties in the story and in yourself as the storyteller. Tell the story over and over. Play with different voices for each character.

2 The story begins long before you start to tell it. Be very aware of the expression on your face before you begin to tell the story, while the audience is set-tling in. The expression on your face either welcomes the audience or makes them feel shut out. If you are already in the room before the audience enters, then welcome them by acknowledging them with a smile or a nod.

3 Imagine that you and the audi-ence are in a safe, loving, gold-en circle outside normal time and place.

4 Your eyes are a powerful story-telling tool. Where you look is where the audience will look. So, when a character is speaking, always look at that character.

5 The role of the "Narrator" is actually a character in the story. Change the expression on your face when being the Narrator.

6 When you are acting as Narrator, sweep your eyes over the eyes of the audience to bring them into the story. Use the expression on your face to "com-ment" on the action of the story. For instance, a slightly raised eye-brow will say to your audience – "Can you believe that he's going to do that?!"

7 Most of the time, we don't breathe deeply enough to sup-port and sustain our voices. Imagine that there is a column of air that goes through the center of your body from the top of your head to the tip of your toes. When you breathe in, let your tummy relax, and let the air flow into that empty column just as water fills a tall vase.

8 Stand or sit tall so you can breathe well.

9 The space between words and phrases is actually as powerful as the words themselves. The spaces between the words establish the rhythm and timing of the story. Use the spaces to connect with the audience. Give the story time, and room, to breathe.

10 Play with the volume control on your voice. Even when you are speaking softly, the audience still needs to hear every word. You may wish to invest in a microphone. I wear a wireless headset microphone for my shows, and love it.

11 Think about the shape of your voice. You want your voice to be rich, chocolaty, warm, and welcoming. Luckily, just paying attention to your voice will help to make it richer and fuller.

12 Learn to change the pace of the story. Think about the movements in a symphony. Some are fast and some are slow. Some move back and forth like a tennis ball.

13 Learn to read the cues an audience is giving you. Even though you are the one who is speaking, they are communicating to you, and you will need to adjust your performance to meet them. Sometimes, though, it will just bomb. Wah! It happens to us all. Get over it, learn from it, and keep polishing … you'll get it, if you keep working on it.

14 Humor is very important in storytelling. One way of achieving humor is to lead audiences in one direction, making them think that the narrative is going a certain way, and then offer a totally unexpected shift in direction. Humor can also be created by the careful repetition of phrases or motifs; use them as you would a delicious spice.

Performing with the Woven Beanstalk Dolls

The Jack and the Beanstalk Dolls that I've designed for you to weave are very small. This means that they will work best when you are telling the story to small groups.

While you are developing your interpretation of the story, here's a useful exercise that you can play with: Try telling the story from another character's viewpoint, and make that character the hero. Think how different the story is when it's told from the Harp's viewpoint instead of Jack's. You'll be amazed at what you learn about the characters when you do this. It's really fun!

How are you the most comfortable when telling the story?

Do you prefer to stand or to sit? Try both to see which works best for you.

Having pins on the back of each doll's head makes them easier to manipulate, and allows you to wear them, too.

If you are not comfortable holding the dolls while telling the story, you might sew them to a vest, hat, coat, bag, or wall hanging and tell the story while pointing to the different characters.

Extra props: Chocolate coins in gold foil are fun to use as the Giant's gold, and a cloth hanky is useful as a blanket or hiding place for Jack. Sometimes you can "make believe" the prop. For instance, the beans could easily be invisible.

People will ask about how you made the dolls. Bring your loom along and, after the story, explain how you wove the dolls. Encourage your audience – convince them that they can also weave dolls and stories!

Looms: The Beanstalk Loom or Potholder Loom

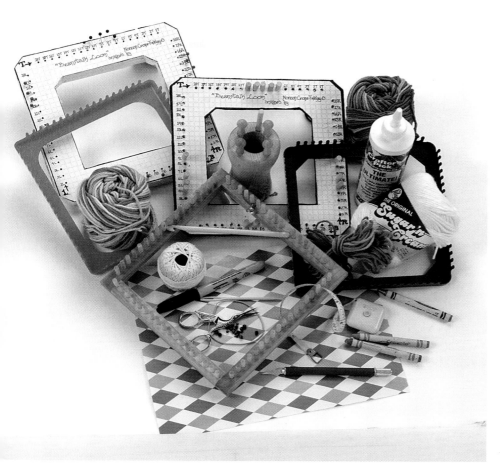

The Beanstalk Dolls are woven on potholder looms or the "beanstalk loom." Potholder looms are approximately 7-1/2" square. They have 18 pegs along each side. They are made of metal, wood, or plastic. (Please refer to the "Sources and Suppliers" section of the book on page 13.)

It is very helpful to number the pegs on your loom, if you are working with a standard potholder loom. Use a permanent black, fine-tip pen, using the beanstalk loom as a guide. Please refer to the pattern for the beanstalk loom to see how the pegs are numbered. The first peg on the vertical sides of the loom is at the bottom, and the first peg on the horizontal sides of the loom is at the right hand side.

The pattern and directions for the beanstalk loom are on page 14. To weave on the beanstalk loom, insert pegs in the holes that are listed in the pattern, and warp them according to directions.

No Tools? No Problem!

If you don't have access to a saw and drill, you may wish to use the pattern for the beanstalk loom as a pinboard loom. You simply lay the pattern on dense construction foam (available from the hardware store) or layers of foam core board (available from the stationery store) or on layers of corrugated cardboard, and glue it in place. Insert pins at the dots, instead of pegs. Be sure to insert the pins at an angle. Use glass-headed pins, or even regular pins, but not 'T' pins.

Tools and Materials to Weave the Beanstalk Dolls

Darning needles
-to weave the heads and bodies of the dolls.

Needle and thread
-to sew on beads.

Crochet hook
-(6 mm or "J") to weave the arm strands through the body warp strands.

Scissors or thread snipper

Measuring tape or ruler

2 rubber bands
-to stretch across the loom as guides for changing colors or for shaping the weaving.

Fabric glue
-permanent water-proof glue –my favorite is The Ultimate™ by Crafter's Pick.

Crayon or pencil crayon
-red or pink for cheeks, green for the Giants, gold for the Harp.

Yarn
-the dolls in this book have been woven with Lily Sugar 'N Cream Cotton™. Other yarns of similar weight can be substituted. Small amounts of each color is required; small amounts of pink and black yarn for features.

Pin backs or small safety pins
-1 for each doll and 2 for Milky White.
-1 small bell for Milky White's neck.

Paper
-8-1/2" x 5" heavy weight paper (such as watercolor paper or business card stock) for the Harp, and 1 piece of plain white paper.

Strong white thread
-such as crochet cotton or dental floss, for the strings of the harp.

2 chenille stems
-white, for Milky White.

Beads
-each doll needs two small black seed beads for eyes. Milky White needs beads that are about 1/8" diameter.

Sources and Suppliers

The woven Beanstalk dolls are all made with Lily Sugar 'N Cream yarn.

www.sugarncream.com

Beautiful metal potholder looms:

http://www.harrisville.com/html/friendlyloompdts.html

Lovely wooden potholder looms and beautiful wooden spoolknitters:

http://www.cedarhollow.net/html/pr_looms.html

Cheap and cheerful red plastic potholder looms:

www.dickblick.com/zz650/01/products.asp?param=0&ig_id=2251

My favorite fabric glue: "The Ultimate!" from Crafter's Pick.

www.crafterspick.com

Wooden cribbage board pegs and a really great awl for piercing holes are available from Lee Valley Tools:

www.leevalley.com

Noreen's Web site:

http://www.crone-findlay.com

ONLINE RESOURCES:

The Union Internationale de la Marionette Web site:

http://www.unima.org/

The Puppeteers of America Web site:

http://www.puppeteers.org/

The Storytelling Center:

http://www.storytellingcenter.net/

The Puppetry home page:

http://www.sagecraft.com

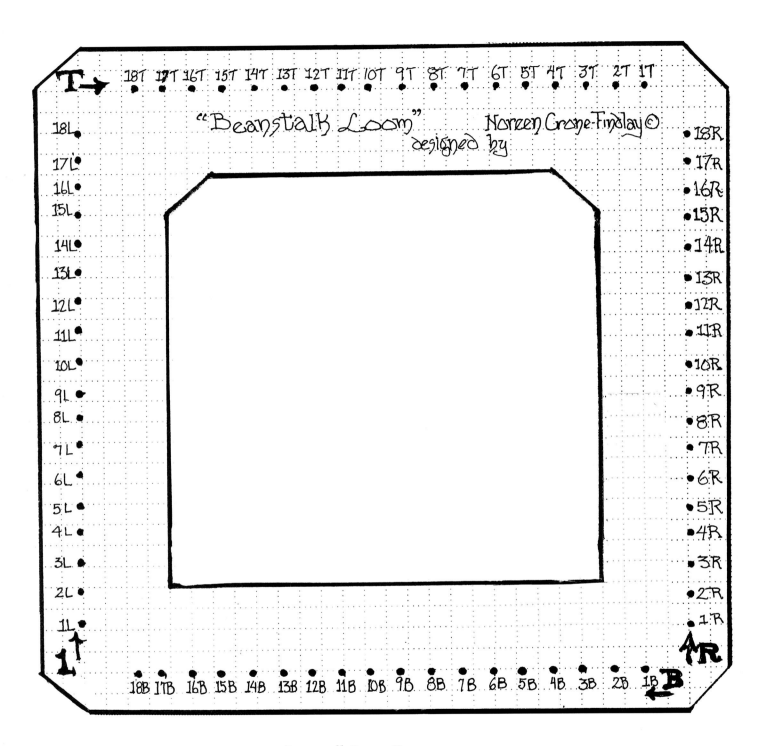

T→

18T 17T 16T 15T 14T 13T 12T 11T 10T 9T 8T 7T 6T 5T 4T 3T 2T 1T

"Beanstalk Loom"   Noreen Crone-Findlay ©
designed by

18L   18R
17L   17R
16L   16R
15L   15R
14L   14R
13L   13R
12L   12R
11L   11R
10L   10R
9L   9R
8L   8R
7L   7R
6L   6R
5L   5R
4L   4R
3L   3R
2L   2R
1L   1R

1↑   ↑R

18B 17B 16B 15B 14B 13B 12B 11B 10B 9B 8B 7B 6B 5B 4B 3B 2B 1B   B

Beanstalk Loom Pattern
Enlarge to 110%

Materials to Make the Beanstalk Loom

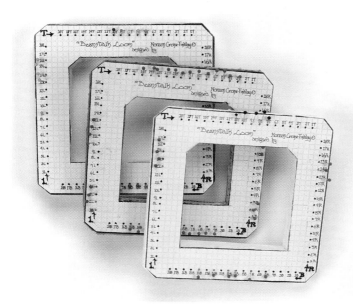

You Will Need:

An 8" x 8" square of hardboard (1/8" thick medium density fiberboard – smooth on both sides)

A saw or sharp craft knife and a drill or sharp awl

Paint for the back of the loom (optional)

40 pegs (I broke some of mine when I was wheedling them into the holes, so you might want to buy a few extra pegs). If you wish to use the beanstalk loom like a regular potholder loom, then you will need 72 pegs. The pegs can be plastic cribbage board pegs or wooden ones. (See Sources and Suppliers section, page 13.)

Glue

Directions:

1 Enlarge and copy pattern. Glue to hardboard. Allow to dry.

2 Cut out loom. Cut out center section. You can use a scroll saw or a sharp craft knife.

3 Paint back of loom, or glue decorative paper to it. Cover front of loom with a couple of coats of white glue to seal it. Paint edges of loom black.

4 Drill holes at dots with a drill or awl.

Materials to Make a Pinboard Loom

You Will Need:

A sharp craft knife

A ruler

One 8" x 8" square of dense construction insulation foam (from the hardware store)

OR:

3 squares of foam core board (from the stationery store) or corrugated cardboard (from a cardboard box)

Glue (I used white craft glue that dries clear)

Glass headed pins

Directions:

1 Enlarge and copy the pattern; glue it to the insulation foam and cut it out.

OR:

2 Cut three squares of foam core that are 8" square. Glue them together. Copy the pattern and glue it to the top layer of foam core board. When the glue is completely dry, cut out the center. The boards have a tendency to separate when they're drying, so put a plastic bag on them, and a stack of phone books.

OR:

3 Cut three squares of corrugated cardboard that are 8" square each. Glue them together, having the center layer at a right angle to the top and bottom layers for added strength (the top and bottom layer corrugations will run top to bottom, and the layer in the middle will have its corrugations running side to side). Copy the pattern and glue it to the layer of foam core board. When dry, cut out the center.

4 Spread a coat of white glue over surface to protect it.

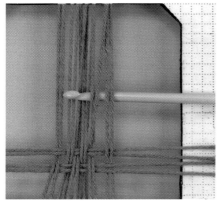

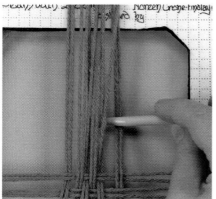

Abbreviations

U: Under – pass yarn, crochet hook or darning needle under the number of strands listed. (i.e.: U4 means go under four strands).

O: Over – pass yarn, crochet hook or darning needle over the number of strands listed. (i.e.: O2 means go over two strands).

T: Top edge of loom.

R: Right hand side of loom.

B: Bottom edge of loom.

L: Left hand side of loom.

NUMBER FOLLOWED BY A LETTER: Indicates peg number and side of loom that the peg is on.

A Note About Constructing the Dolls

The bodies and heads of the dolls are woven with a blunt darning needle. The arms are woven through the body strands with a crochet hook. The warp strands that form the arms and legs of the dolls are wrapped with yarn to shape them.

Warping the Loom

"Warp" means the strands of yarn that form the foundation of the weaving. "Warping" is the process of going from peg to peg to lay out the foundation of the doll. The body warp strands go from the top to the bottom edge of the loom. Changing the position of the arm warps changes the proportion of the doll.

NOTE: SOME OF THE DOLLS ARE WARPED WITH JUST ONE STRAND OF YARN, AND SOME ARE WARPED WITH TWO STRANDS HELD TOGETHER.

If you are using a single strand of yarn to warp the loom, you will be weaving O2, U2.

If you are using two strands held together, you will weave O4, U4.

Weaving the Beanstalk Dolls

Jack

Finished height of doll is approximately 4-3/4".

You Will Need:

Small amounts of Lily Sugar 'N Cream:
  Skin color: Jute;
  Body color: Country Brown, Ombre.
A few inches of pink yarn for mouth, and black for trim.
2 small beads for eyes

(If you are using the Beanstalk Loom, you will insert pegs in 7T, 8T, 9T, 10T, 11T, 7B, 8B, 9B, 10B, 11B, 12B, 12L, 10L, 9L, 8L, 7L, 5L, 12R, 9R, 8R, 7R, 5R.)

Directions:

1 HEAD AND BODY: When warping, do not pull yarn tight! With one strand of body color yarn, warp loom. Tie the end of the yarn to the top edge of the loom in space between pegs 7T and 8T.

2 Go around the following pegs in this order (Note: Yarn goes around some pegs on "T" twice); 7B, 8T, 8B, 8T, 9B, 9T, 10B, 9T, 11B, 10T, 12B, take yarn up to top edge of loom, through space between 10T & 11T.

3 ARMS: Take yarn around the back of loom. Bring the yarn up to the front of loom in space between 10L and 9L.

4 With crochet hook, starting at right hand side of warp strands, weave hook O2, U2, O2, U2, O2, U2. The business-end of hook is now close to left edge of the loom.

5 Place yarn on hook, and pull through warp strands.

6 Place loop on peg 9R.

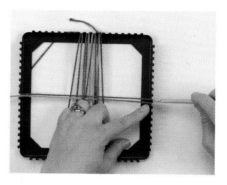

7 Yarn has passed between rows 10 L & 9L.

8 Place the hook below the horizontal strands, & beginning on the right, weave hook U2, O2, U2, O2, U2, O2. Place yarn on hook, taking it past peg 9L, and pull through warp strands.

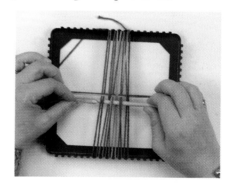

9 Place loop 8R.

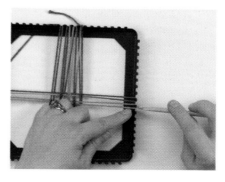

10 Weave hook: O2, U2, O2, U2, O2, U2.

Place yarn on hook, taking it past peg 8L, and pull through warp strands. Place loop on peg 7R.

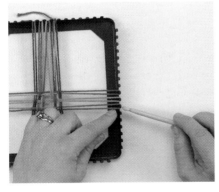

Cut the warp yarn 60" past peg 7L. This yarn will be used to weave the body and wrap the first leg. Wrap it around the loom for now, to keep it out of the way while you weave the head.

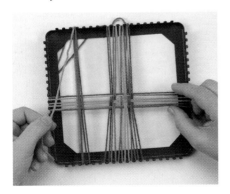

11 JACK'S HEAD: Place a rubber band around loom in space above twelfth side pegs. This is the guideline for the top of the head.

12 SHAPING THE NECK: Cut a 36" length of skin tone yarn. Pull up the ends until they are even and tie a knot. Push knot over to right hand side of neck.

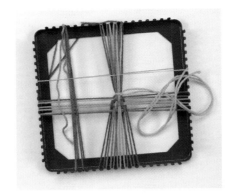

13 WEAVING THE FACE: Thread ends into darning needle, and weave with two strands held together, beginning at right hand side. Do not pull hard on the yarn. It needs to be rather loose in order to pack down and cover warp strands. First row: *O5, U4, O3.

Next row: U3, O4, U5*.

Repeat from * to *, up to the rubber band. Push rows down firmly as you weave to cover warp strands completely. Take the rubber band off the loom.

14 Wrap the yarn around all the warp strands at top of head, pulling in to shape it. Thread the darning needle down through head to bury the skin-tone yarn end. Snip ends close to weaving.

15 WEAVING THE BODY: Place a rubber band around loom in space above fourth side pegs. This is the guideline for switching from weaving the body to wrapping legs.

16 Turn loom upside down, to weave from arms toward feet.

17 Bring the 60"-long strand of yarn past peg 7L. Fold it so the cut end is just slightly past edge of body. Thread the fold into the darning needle.

18 Weave O2, U2 up to rubber band. Pull up on yarn as you weave so body is about 1" wide. End at side "L" of loom. Remove the rubber band.

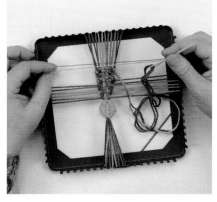

19 FIRST LEG: WRAPPING YARN: Turn loom again, so the body and leg warp strands are horizontal and the arms are vertical. Lift loops off pegs 12B, 11B, and 10B.

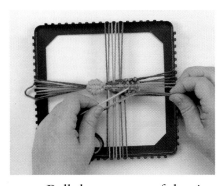

20 Pull the yarn out of darning needle and snip at the fold. Take one yarn end to the center and set aside to wrap the second leg. Wrap the yarn around the loose leg loops, up to the last 1/2".

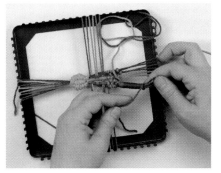

21 Push the wraps toward the body to make them dense. Put a dab of fabric glue along the "foot" warp strands.

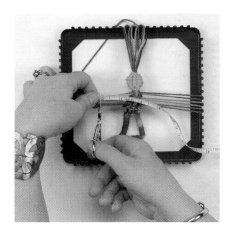

22 Fold the loops over and pull up a little on the wrapping yarn, then wrap to the toe of the foot, squishing the yarn into the glue. The heel of the foot will not be wrapped. Be sure to fold the foot so that it is sticking out in front of the body.

23 With the remaining length of yarn, wrap the second leg from the hip to the toe, shaping the foot in the same way as the first leg.

24 WRAPPING YARN AROUND THE ARMS: Snip the arm warp strands 1-1/2" from body. Untie the yarn at peg 7T, and lift the doll off the loom.

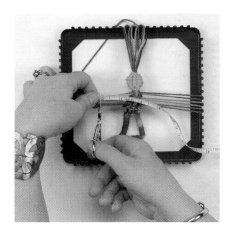

25 Lay the end of the yarn from the ball onto the first arm, with the end of the yarn at the fingertips. Wrap the arm strands beginning at the shoulder, for 1".

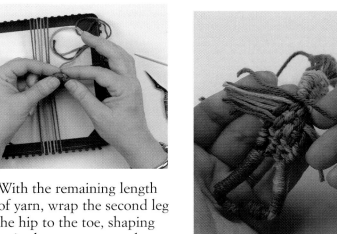

26 Snip the body color. Put a dab of fabric glue on the warp strands. Push the end of the body color into the glue.

27 Push the end of the hand color yarn into the glue, then start wrapping the yarn around the hand, right up against

the last round of sleeve color. Wrap up to the fingertips, then press the skin color into glue, and snip the end.

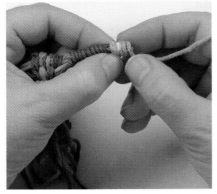

28 Repeat for the other arm.

29 HAIR: Use long warp ends from the top of loom for hair around the doll's face by threading them, one at a time, into darning needle, and embroidering straight stitches on the doll's forehead and at the sides of the face.

30 Trim warp loops at the top of the head to 1/2" long. Use the cut-off ends to cover the back of the head by gluing in place on the back of the head. Trim ends.

Finishing

1 Sew two small black seed beads onto the face for eyes.

2 Embroider the mouth with pink yarn. Make two short straight stitches, one on top of the other for the mouth.

3 Rub a small amount of pink crayon on the cheeks.

4 LACING UP THE FRONT OF JACK'S SHIRT: Cut a piece of thin black yarn 12" long. Thread one end into the darning needle. Being careful to only go through the top layer of the doll and starting at lower edge of body, take a horizontal stitch. Bring the ends of the yarn up even.

5 With one end only in the darning needle, go through one strand of the body three times so they zigzag up front of the body.

6 Place each one so they are about 1/4" long. Each stitch makes half of an "X." Pull the yarn out of the darning needle, and thread the other end into the darning needle. Make three more stitches to finish the "X's."

7 Tie a bow just below the chin. Trim ends, and glue down.

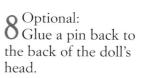

8 Optional: Glue a pin back to the back of the doll's head.

Mother

Finished height of doll is approximately 5-1/2".

You Will Need:

Small amounts of Lily Sugar 'N Cream:
    Body: Countryside Ombre
    Skin: Cream
    Collar: White, 15"
2 small beads for eyes

Directions:

If you are using the beanstalk loom, you will insert pegs in 7T, 8T, 9T, 10T, 11T, 7B, 8B, 9B, 10B, 11B, 12B, 15L, 13L, 12L, 11L, 10L, 6L, 15R, 12R, 11R, 10R, 6R.

1 WARPING THE HEAD AND BODY: With one strand of body color yarn, warp the loom from the upper to the lower edge in the same way as you did for Jack.

2 WARPING THE ARMS: Warp the arms just like Jack's, although Mother's arms are higher and longer than Jack's. The warp comes up between pegs 13L and l2L and goes onto pegs 12L, 11L, 12R, 11R, and 10R. When you take it past peg 10L, measure 120" of yarn, then snip. Wrap this around the loom while weaving the head.

3 Place a rubber band in the space above pegs 15R & 15L and another in the space above pegs 6L & 6R.

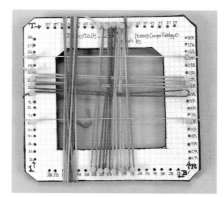

4 HEAD: Weave Mother's head exactly the same as Jack's. Her head is between the top strand of arms at pegs 13 and the rubber band above pegs 15.

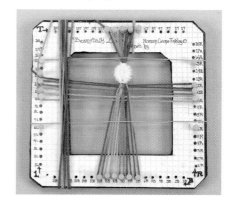

5 WEAVING THE BODY:
Turn the loom so pegs "B" are at top of loom. Unwrap the 120" length of yarn and fold in half. Have the end of yarn at the edge of the body. Thread the fold into the darning needle and weave, Row 1: O4, U4, O4 and Row 2:U4, O4, U4. Repeat from * to * to the rubber band. Shape the dress by pulling in under arms and widening as the dress progresses to the hem.

Now, switch to *Row l: O2, U2, O2, U2, O2, U2. Row 2: O2, U2, O2, U2, O2, U2*. Repeat from * to * to the hem of the dress. Last row: O1, U2, O2, U2, O2, U2, O1. Take the end up inside the dress.

6 WRAPPING ARMS: Wrap Mother's arms in the same way as Jack's, but make her arms 2" long. 1-1/2" body color, 1/2" skin tone. Lift the doll off the loom.

Finishing

1 Finish the face just like Jack's.

2 HAIR: Wrap 30" of blue yarn around two fingers.

3 Cut a short piece of yarn, and pass it through the loops, then tie a knot to secure them.

4 Glue the loops to top of the back of the doll's head.

5 Fold the warp loops from the top of the head down the sides of the doll's face and glue in place.

6 COLLAR: Cut a piece of white yarn 15" long. Fold it in half and thread ends through a darning needle. Take the darning needle through one horizontal stitch at the doll's front waist, being careful to only go through the top layer of the doll.

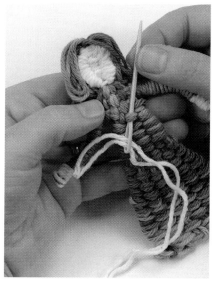

7 Leave a tail of an inch, and go over one shoulder, taking a stitch at the back of the doll's waist. Go through the same horizontal stitch twice.

8 Come back over the other shoulder, and go through the same stitch at the front.

9 Tie a half-knot. Trim ends, and glue down.

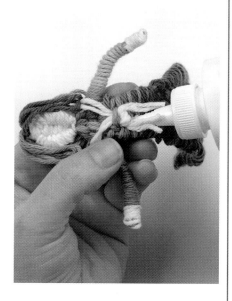

10 Optional: Glue a pin back to the back of the doll's head.

Giantess

Finished height of Giantess doll is approximately 7".

You Will Need:

Small amounts of Lily Sugar 'N Cream:
 Body: Country Sage Ombre
 Skin: Celadon
2 small beads for eyes

Directions:

(If you are using the beanstalk loom, you will insert pegs in 7T, 8T, 9T, 10T, 11T, 5B, 7B, 9B, 10B, 12 B, 14B, 16L, 15L, 14L, 13L, 15R 14R, 13R.

1 HEAD AND BODY: With two strands of ombre yarn, warp the loom the same way as the Mother doll. If you are using the beanstalk loom, treat the pegs on "B" as if they were in the same place as the Mother warping plan.

2 On a regular potholder loom, the Giantess' skirt is made wider by lifting warp loops and placing them onto the following pegs:

Lift loop on peg 7B & place onto peg 5B.

Lift loop on peg 8B & place onto peg 7B.

Lift loop on peg 12B & place onto peg 14B.

Lift loop on peg 11B & place onto peg 12B.

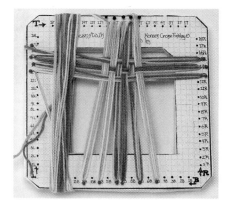

3 ARMS: NOTE: The arms are made just like Jack's, but higher on the loom. Take the yarn through the space between pegs 11T and 10T, around the back of the loom and up to the front of loom at the space between pegs 16L and 15L. You will have loops of warp on pegs 15R, 14R, and 13R, and loops of warp on pegs 15L and 14L. Measure 175" from peg 13L for the skirt, (two strands) and wrap around the loom to keep it out of the way while you weave the head.

4 GIANTESS' HEAD: NOTE: Do not pull in at the neck. Cut a 60" length of pale green skin-tone yarn. Thread one end into a darning needle and, starting at the right hand side, go U6, then pull the ends up even and thread the second end into the needle. Now: O8, U6, O4.

Row l: *U4, O6, U8, O6.

Row 2: U6, O8, U6, O4*.

Repeat from * to * to top of the loom.

Push the rows down firmly as you weave to cover the warp strands.

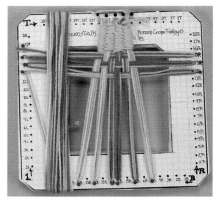

5 WEAVING THE SKIRT: Thread ends of the 175" length of yarn into darning needle. Take yarn past peg 13L to begin:

Weave: U4, O4, U4, O4, U4, O4. Repeat this row up to the hem.

At the hem, weave: U2, O4, U4, O4, U4, O4, U2.

Next row:O2, U4, O4, U4, O4, U4, O2.

Take the needle up inside weaving, snip end.

6 SHAPING TOP OF HEAD: Untie the starting yarn, and snip the end that passes behind the loom. Thread the starting yarn into the darning needle and take the darning needle through all the loops on pegs 8T, 9T & 10T. Take the other end through in the opposite direction. Tie a knot with the other loose end to shape the top of the head. Do not snip the ends, as they will be used to tie the hair to the head. Lift the Giantess doll off the loom.

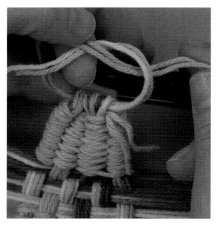

7 WRAPPING THE YARN AROUND THE ARMS: Arms are wrapped in the same way as Jack's, except they are worked all the way to the end. Wrap arms in body color. The last 1/2" is wrapped with skin tone.

Finishing

1 NOSE: Cut one strand of green yarn 12" long, thread it into the darning needle and bring down through the weaving from the top of the head. Bring the darning needle out at the center of the face, two or three stitches down from top of the head. Call this point "A."

2 Take the needle back into the head, 1/2" down from point "A." Call this point "B."

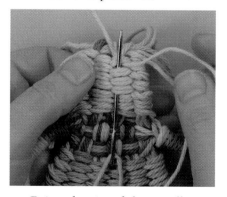

3 Bring the tip of the needle out at "A," and wrap the yarn around the tip of the needle nine times.

4 Pull the needle through all the wraps, and go back into the head at point "B," coming out at the top of the head. Tie a knot with the starting end, and snip.

5 Sew two small black seed beads onto the face for eyes.

6 Embroider the mouth with dark brown or black yarn.

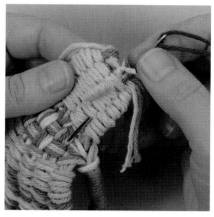

Go down through the top of the head, across for the mouth, up through the head.

Tie a knot, trim ends.

7 Rub dark green crayon on cheeks and above eyes.

8 HAIR: Wrap 40" of body yarn around three fingers, forming loops.

Cut the loops open then lay them on the knot on top of the head. Tie a knot at the center of the strands to secure them.

Secure hair to the head with glue. Trim ends.

9 Optional: Stitch or glue a pin back to the doll.

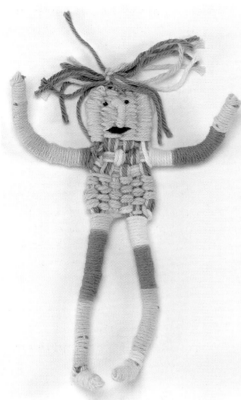

Giant

Finished height of Giant doll is approximately 7".

WARPING THE BODY: The Giant is warped with two strands of yarn held together.

Directions:

If you are using the beanstalk loom, insert pegs in 7T, 8T, 9T, 10T, 11T, 7B, 8B, 9B, 10B, 11B, 12B, 16L, 15L, 14L, 13L, 9L, 15R, 14R, 13R, 9R.

You Will Need:

The Giant uses the same materials as the Giantess.

1 HEAD AND BODY: When warping, do not pull yarn tight! With two strands of body-color yarn, warp the loom: Tie the end of the yarn to the top edge of the loom in space between pegs 7T and 8T.

2 Go around the following pegs in this order: 7B, 8T, 8B, 8T, 9B, 9T, 10B, 9T, 11B, 10T, 12B, take the yarn up to the top edge of the loom through space between 10T & 11T. Place a rubber band in the space above peg 9.

3 ARMS: NOTE: The arms are made just like Jack's, but higher on the loom. Take the yarn through the space between pegs 11T and 10T, around the back of the loom and up to the front of the loom at the space between pegs 16L and 15L. You will have loops of warp on pegs 15R, 14R, and 13R. There will be loops of warp on pegs 15L and 14L. Measure 80" from peg 13L for the body and the first leg, (two strands) and wrap around the loom to keep it out of the way while you weave the head.

4 Weave the head in same way as Giantess.

5 Weave the Giant's body: U4, O4, U4, O4, U4, O4, repeating this row to the rubber band.

6 Wrap the Giant's legs the same way as Jack's, wrapping to last 1/4". Glue the end of the wrapped yarn to the legs, leaving loops at end of leg exposed. Feet will be added.

7 FOOT: Cut a 20" length of skin tone yarn (pale green), fold it in half, and thread into the darning needle. Hold a finger against the end of the leg. Stitch over your finger, through the end of leg loops five times.

8 Dab glue along the foot loops and wrap with remaining yarn. Pinch the toe into a point.

9 Finish the Giant's arms, face, and hair the same as the Giantess.

10 Optional: Glue a pin back to back of the doll's head.

Beanman

Finished height of Beanman is approximately 4-1/2".

You Will Need:

Lily Sugar 'N Cream:
  Body & Hat: Sage
  Skin tone: Jute
  Hair: White
2 small beads for eyes

Directions:

If you are using the beanstalk loom, insert pegs in 7T, 8T, 9T, 10T, 11T, 7B, 8B, 9B, 10B, 11B, 12 B, 9L, 6L, 5L, 4L, 9R, 6R, 5R.

1 With one strand body color, warp the body and head in the same way as for Jack. Place a rubber band in the space above pegs 9.

2 There are only two sets of warp strands for arms: Bring first arm warp out in the space between 6L and 5L. Place the warp onto pegs 6R and 5R. Cut the yarn 28" past peg 4L. It will come around peg 4L to begin weaving.

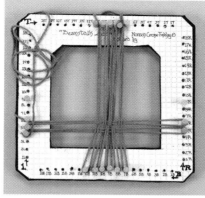

3 HEAD: Cut 30" skin tone. Take one end U4 strands at the right hand side above the arms. Bring the ends up even and thread into a darning needle.
  Weave: O4, U4.
  Next Row: *O4, U4, O4.
  Next Row: U4, O4, U4*.
  Repeat from * to *, up to the rubber band, pulling in to shape the head. At the rubber band, take the skin-tone yarn into the head. Snip ends.

4 WEAVE THE BODY: Thread the yarn at peg 4L into a darning needle, and take past 4L. Weave U2 O2 for four rows for the body, pulling in so that the body is about an inch wide.

5 WRAP ARMS and LEGS the same as you did for Jack. Note: Arms are 1-1/4" long.

6 HAT: Cut a short length of thread or yarn.

7 Use the short length of yarn to tie a tight knot around the loops half way between the ends of the loops and the Beanman's forehead. Stroke the ends of the knot into the loops. Fold the loops from the top of the loom down to the back of the head so that the end of the loops touches the back of the neck. Use a scrap of yarn to stitch the loops in place at the nape of his neck.

8 WRAP THE HAT: Push the end of the yarn from the ball into the hat loops.

9 Run a bead of fabric glue along the hat loops.

10 Wrap the hat loops from the forehead up to the point of the hat, pulling in and shaping the yarn as you go. Snip the end of the yarn, and glue the end to the hat.

Finishing

1 Sew two small black seed beads onto the face for eyes.

2 HAIR: Wrap white yarn around two fingers 30 times. Snip the loops open. Fold them in half and glue or stitch to head.

3 EYEBROWS: Take white yarn through the head from back to front and make one short straight stitch above the eye, going through to the back.

Come up through from the back to the front and make a second eyebrow over the other eye.

4 NOSE: Insert the point of a darning needle into a horizontal stitch at the center of the face and tug on it a little to raise it up from the face.

5 MUSTACHE: Bring a needle through the face, from the back of the head to the front, and make a stitch, going through the head from front to back. Make six vertical stitches in this manner under the nose.

6 Optional: Glue a pin back to the back of the doll's head.

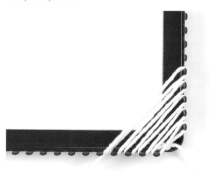

The Hen

Finished height of Hen doll is approximately 1-1/2".

You Will Need:

Small amounts of Lily Sugar 'N Cream:
White, Red, Pumpkin
2 small beads for eyes

The Hen is made by weaving a small triangle and folding it in half.

NOTE: If you are using the beanstalk loom, then insert pegs into: 5B, 4B, 3B, 2B, 1B, 5R, 4R, 3R, 2R, & 1 R.

Directions:

1 Tie one strand of white yarn to peg 1B, then take the yarn around the following pegs in this order: 1R, 1B, 2R, 2B, 3R, 3B, 4R, 4B, 5R, 5B.

2 Measure 54" of yarn from peg 5B. Snip. Thread the end into a darning needle.

3 The triangle is woven with a pattern of eight short rows, which is repeated four times. Begin with the darning needle at peg 5B:
    *R l: O2,U2,O2,U2,O2.

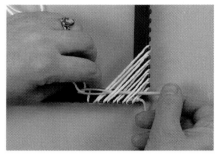

R 2: U2, O2, U2, O2, U2.
R 3: O2, U2, O2, U2.
R 4: O2, U2, O2, U2.
R 5: O2, U2, O2.
R 6: U2, O2, U2.
R 7: O2, U2*.
R 8: O2, U2.

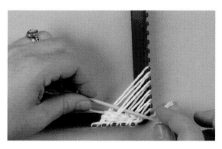

4 Repeat from * to * three more times.

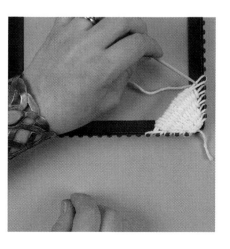

5 After the fourth repeat of the pattern, weave: O1, U2, O2, U2, O2, U1.

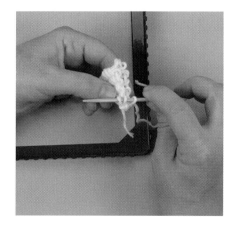

6 Lift the triangle off the loom.

7 Fold the triangle in half. Sew the loopy edges together.

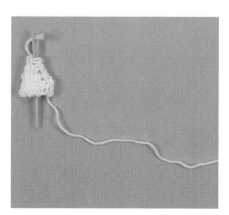

8 The point at the top of the triangle is the head. Take the yarn end at the top of the head inside the Hen.

9 TAIL: Stitch 1/2" long loops at the center back seam on the lower edge of the Hen.

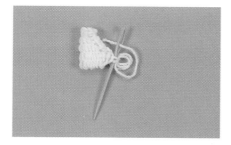

10 Cut a 10"-long piece of white yarn and stitch more tail loops.

11 Put a dab of glue into the base of the loops to hold in place.

12 EYES: Sew two small black seed beads to the head for eyes. Stitch through the Hen's head to secure the beads.

13 BEAK: With one strand of orange yarn, take a couple of small loops at the front of the face.

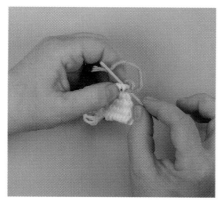

Put a dab of glue onto the beak, and pinch and squeeze it to shape the beak.

14 COMB AND WATTLE: Cut 10" of red yarn. Bring it up through the top of the head and stitch one small stitch in place to anchor it. Stitch four small 1/4" long loops at the top of the head. Take out under the beak, and stitch two loops that are approximately 1/2" long under the beak.

Glue the end of the red yarn inside the body.

15 WINGS: Cut a length of white yarn 18" long and thread one end into a darning needle. Go through one stitch on the side of the Hen, pull up the ends even, and thread the second end through the darning needle.

16 Stitch over a finger to form a loop then make a smaller stitch to lock the loop in place.

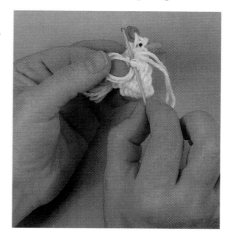

17 Take the darning needle through to the other side and make second wing in the same way as the first.

18 Take the ends inside the Hen and weave in along the lower edge.

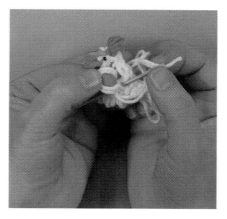

19 Optional: Glue a pin back to one side of the Hen.

The Golden Egg

1 First, buy a chocolate bar that is wrapped in gold-colored foil.

2 Eat chocolate bar.

3 Shape a small piece of aluminum foil into an egg-shape.

4 Cover with the gold foil.

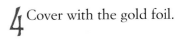

Repeat steps 1 and 2 as often as necessary.

Milky White, The Cow

Finished size of Milky White is 6-1/2" long by 3-1/2" high.

You Will Need:

Lily Sugar 'N Cream:
White and Tea Rose
2 white chenille stems
2 black beads, 1/8"
Small bell for neck and a ribbon or piece of yarn to tie it on

NOTE: Milky White has a different warping pattern than the people Beanstalk Dolls. While you are weaving her, she looks like a bearskin rug. Later, she'll be folded in half along her spine and will be free standing.

If you are using the beanstalk loom, then insert pegs in: 3T, 4T, 5T, 6T, 7T, 8T, 9T, 10T, 11T, 12T, 13T, 14T, 15T, 13L, 12L, 11L, 10L, 4L, 3L, 2L, 1L, 4B, 5B, 6B, 7B, 8B, 9B, 10B, 11B, 12B, 13B, 14B, 15B, 12R, 11R, 10R, 3R, 2R, and 1R.

Directions:

1 WARPING MILKY WHITE (use two strands of white yarn): Tie the yarn in the space between 3T and 4T. Take the yarn around the following pegs in this order: 4B, 4T, 5B, 5T, 6B, 6T, 7B, 7T, 8B, 8T, 9B, 9T, 10B, 10T, 11B, 11T, 12B, 12T, 13B, 13T, 14B, 14T, 15B, up to the space between 14T and 15T. Then take the yarn around the back of the loom and bring out in the notch between pegs 13L and 12L.

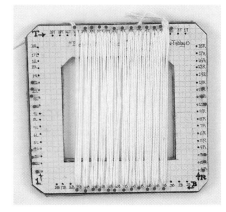

2 You will now warp her "front legs" (on pegs 12, 11, 10). With the hook, weave three sets of warp strands, just the way you did for the "people" doll's arms (remembering to weave U4, O4.). There will be loops of warp around pegs 12R, 11R, and 10R and pegs 12L and 11L.

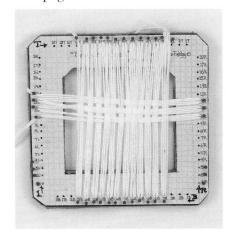

Take the warp through the space between pegs 11L and 10L

and go behind the loom, then bring it up to the space between pegs 1L and 2L. Weave the hind leg, working from pegs 1, then 2 and 3, ending with loops of yarn on pegs 3R, 2R, 1R and 2L. The yarn will come out in the space between pegs 2L and 3L.

3 Measuring from peg 3L, cut a two-strand length of yarn, 85" long. Thread the ends into a darning needle.

4 WEAVING THE BODY: Go around peg 3L then begin weaving the body. Push the lower leg warps right down to the bottom of the loom. Weave (O4, U4 etc.) from the lower leg up to the upper leg.

5 WEAVING THE NECK AND THE HEAD: Snip the yarn at the back of the loom. Untie the tie on the strand of yarn.

6 NARROWING THE WEAVING FOR THE NECK: Lift the loops off pegs 14T and 13T and off pegs 6T, 5T, and 4T.

7 Place a rubber band over the remaining loops at the top edge of the loom to hold them in place.

Starting at right hand side of loom, weave hook O4, U4, O4, U4, O4, U4.

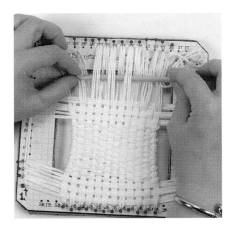

8 Place the loops from pegs 14T and 13T onto the hook and pull them through the warp strands.

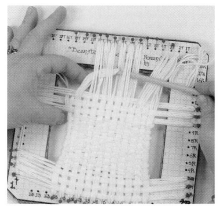

9 With loops still on the hook, take the tie on the yarn through all the loops.

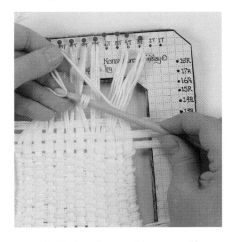

10 Pull the tie on the yarn all the way through the loops and let it hang down the side edge.

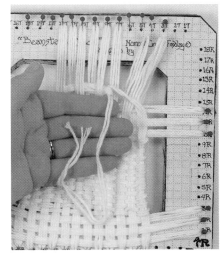

11 Starting at the left hand side, weave hook O4, U4, O4, U4, O4, U4.

12 Place the loops from 6T, 5T, and 4T onto the hook and pull through the warp strands.

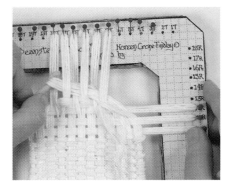

13 Pull the single yarn strand that went over the top of the loom during warping through the loops and let it hang down beside the edge of the weaving.

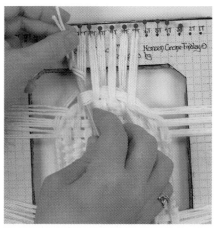

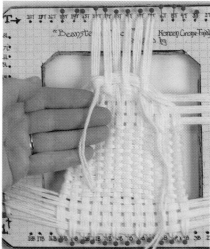

Weaving the Head:

14 WEAVING THE HEAD: Cut an 85" long strand of yarn for the head. Fold it in half and place the loop on the hook.

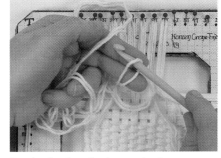

Push the hook through the space in the warp strands that are on pegs 12T and 11T.

Pull the ends all the way through the loop.

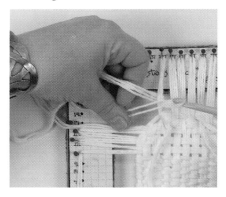

15 Thread the yarn into a darning needle and weave U4, O4 for 1/2".

16 EARS: Place a finger next to the warp strands at peg 7. Take the yarn strands around your finger to form a loop.

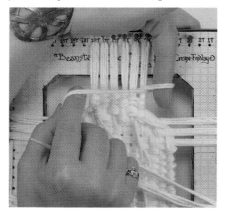

17 Take a stitch through the edge stitch of the row below to secure the loop. (Loop should be about 3/4" long.)

18 Weave back to the other side and make another loop in the same way for other ear, locking it in place with a small stitch as you did for the first ear.

19 Weave O4, U4 etc., until you are about 1" from the top of the loom.

20 Take the rubber band off the loom. Lift loops from 12T onto 11T and 7T onto 8T to shape Milky White's muzzle.

21 Weave to the top of the loom, pulling in slightly to shape the muzzle. You may need to hold the stitches onto the loom with your thumb.

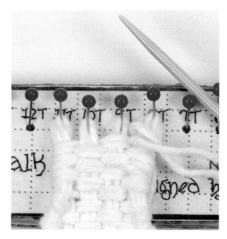

22 LAST ROW: Go through the center of each loop on the pegs and then lift the weaving off the top edge of loom.

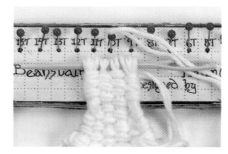

23 Go through the center of the loops once more, and weave the ends into the muzzle.

24 Snip the yarn between pegs 10L and 3L. Lift the weaving off the loom. Trim the ends to the same length as the legs.

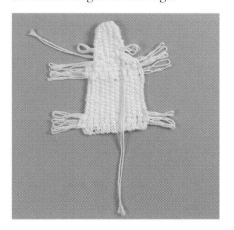

25 WRAPPING THE LEGS: Repeat for all four legs. The legs are wrapped with two strands of yarn coming off the ball. Lay the chenille stem across the cow at the legs. Fold the ends over so that the chenille stem is the same length as the legs.

26 Glue the ends of the yarn from the ball to the cow's body, then wrap the leg strands and chenille stem to 1/2" from the end of the legs.

27 Put a dab of glue on the leg and wrap to the end. Snip the yarn end to 1/8" and glue to the end of the leg.

28 Glue the chenille stems inside the body in place.

29 TAIL: (Note: If there are any loose warp strands along the rump end, cut a length of yarn and stitch through the loops to hold them in place.) Cut four strands of yarn, 4" long. Thread them into a darning needle. Take them through the center point of the lower edge. Bring the ends up even.

30 Glue the end from the ball to the inside of the cow at the rump edge. Wrap the tail up to an inch from the end of the tail.

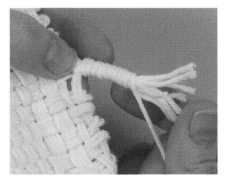

31 The last 1/2" will be the fringe of the tail, so do not put any glue onto it. Put a dab of glue onto the tail, up to the fringe part of tail, and finish winding the strands.

32 Trim the fringe. Feather the fringe ends with the point of the darning needle.

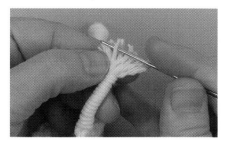

33 FOREHEAD: The forehead is worked on the outside of the cow. Fold the face down at the forehead, from ear to ear. Lay the handle of the crochet hook on the top of the fold.

34 Cut a strand of yarn, 24" long. Fold it in half and glue the ends into the inside of the cow. Thread the fold into the darning needle, and stitch over the crochet hook five or six times, then take the ends inside the cow, and glue in place.

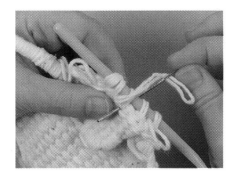

35 Fold the cow in half down her spine. Sew two black 1/4" diameter beads onto the face for eyes. Stitch through the face from bead to bead. Hide the yarn ends inside her muzzle.

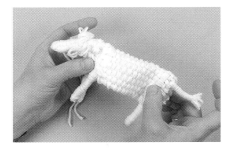

36 NOSE: Put a dab of fabric glue on the last 1/2" of the muzzle and wrap with pink yarn.

37 Put a dab of fabric glue on the end of the nose and glue the ends in, spiraling them into the center.

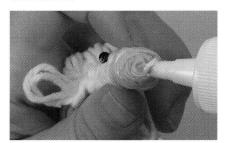

38 EARS: Put a dab of glue on the tip of the ear and pinch to shape it.

39 UDDER: With one strand of pink yarn, weave a triangle in the same way as the Hen.

40 Fold the udder in half, with loopy sides together. Sew the long, "unloopy" ends together.

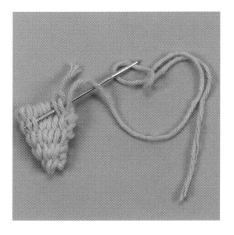

41 Place the udder between the legs and sew the loopy sides to the cow's under belly. Sew the edges of the cow's bottom together.

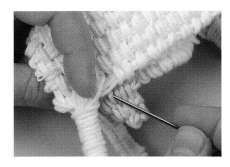

42 BELL: Thread yarn in your choice of colors through a small bell and tie around Milky White's neck.

43 Optional: Glue a pin back to one side of Milky White's head and another to her rump.

Bag for Giant's Gold

Finished size is 2-1/2" x 2".

You Will Need:

**Lily Sugar 'N Cream:
Soft Brown**

If you are using the beanstalk loom, insert pegs in: 7B, 8B, 9B, 10B, 11 B, 12 B, 7T, 8T, 9T, 10T, 11T, 12T.

Directions:

1 Work with one strand of yarn. Tie the yarn in the space between pegs 6T and 7T. Take the yarn around the pegs in this order: 7B, 7T, 8B, 8T, 9B, 9T, 10B, 10T, 11B, 11T, 12B, 12T, and around 12B up through space between 12B and 11B.

2 With the hook at the right-hand side of the loom, just above lower pegs: *Row 1: Weave hook: O1, U2, O2, U2, O2, U2, O2.

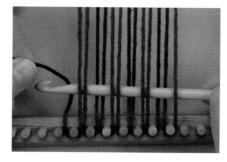

3 Yarn over hook, pull through the warp strands, leave the loop on the hook.

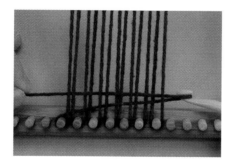

4 Row 2: U1, O2, U2, O2, U2, O2, U2. Yarn over hook, pull through the warp strands and through the loop on the hook; leave the loop on the hook*.

5 Repeat from * to * to the top of the loom. On the last row, take the crochet hook through the center of the warp loops.

6 Untie the yarn and take through the loop on the hook. Snip the yarn from the ball, leaving 10" for joining. Lift the weaving off the loom.

7 Fold one end up for the body of the bag, and sew the side seams. Take the ends inside bag.

8 Fold the other end over for the flap. Place gold coins inside!

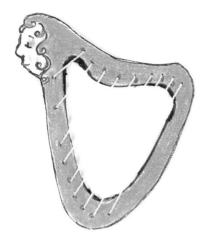

The Harp

Finished size is 2-1/2" x 2".

You Will Need:

Sturdy non-corrugated card stock, 3" x 4"
Glue (The Ultimate by Crafter's Pick)
Scissors
Sharp craft knife
Needle and sturdy thread, such as crochet cotton, perle cotton or dental floss
Gold color crayons, pencil crayons and/or gel pens
Scrap of cardboard or stack of newspaper to use as a cutting surface
Sharp pointed darning needle or awl

Directions:

1 Glue a sheet of plain white paper to one side of the card stock.

2 Copy the Harp onto the paper and glue to the other side of the card stock.

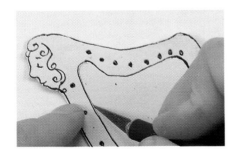

3 When the glue is dry, cut out the Harp with the craft knife. (Lay the scrap cardboard or newspapers under the Harp while cutting to protect the surface you are working on. Also, be sure the knife is very sharp, as a dull knife will skid and slip. Always cut away from yourself.

4 Cut out the second side of the face. Tear the paper where it will join the body of the Harp. This will feather the edges and make them not so noticeable when it's glued to the Harp.

5 Glue the second side of the face to the other side of the Harp.

6 Color the Harp. Outline the edges of the Harp with a black fine tip permanent marker pen.

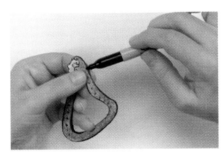

7 With the Harp on a cutting surface, use the awl or a sharp darning needle to pierce the dots for stringing.

8 Thread 20" strong thread into a needle. Starting on the wrong side of the Harp, bring the needle through the Harp, leaving an inch or so of thread on the wrong side.

9 Go across the Harp, and into the hole directly across from the first one.

10 Bring the needle out at the next hole (coming up from back to front), and across to the

next hole. Go through from front to back.

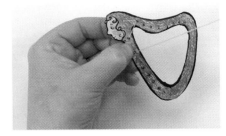

11 Repeat across all holes. Snip end of thread.

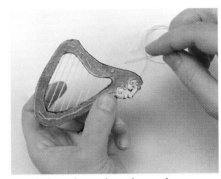

12 Glue thread ends to the Harp, lining them up with stitching.

13 Optional: Glue a pin back to the back of the Harp.

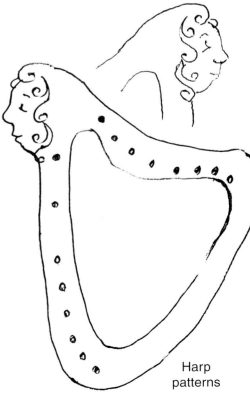

Harp patterns

The Beanstalk

Finished length of each segment is 7-1/2".

You Will Need:

Lily Sugar 'N Cream Dark Pine

If you are using the beanstalk loom: Insert pegs into: 9B, 10B, and 9T.

Directions:

1 TO START THE STEM: Tie two strands of green yarn onto the loom in space between 9B and 10B. Take the yarn up to and around 9T, then down to 9B, and around 9T again.

2 Bring the yarn past 9B and around it. Now, with two strands coming off the ball, wrap the warp strands. Pass the ball around the warp strands five times. (The ball of yarn goes into the loom in the back, comes up through to the front.)

3 TO FORM A LEAF: Push the crochet hook through the center of the stem strands, and pull up a loop of yarn that is about 3/4" long.

4 Pinch the leaf to hold it in place while you wrap the stem strands five more times. Push the wraps down the stem to pack them tightly.

5 Repeat steps 3 and 4, alternately pushing the hook through the stem strands from the right and left hand sides. This will place the leaves on both sides of the stem.

6 Continue until the beanstalk is wrapped right up to the top of the loom.

7 Snip the yarn, then thread the ends into a darning needle. Lift the loops off peg 9T. Take the

ends through the loops from peg 9T, twice.

8 Untie the yarn at the lower edge of the loom, and thread it into the darning needle. Lift the loops off peg 9B then take the darning needle through the loops twice.

9 Make at least two more Beanstalk sections. Use the yarn ends at each end to stitch the sections together.

10 Take all the loose ends inside the Beanstalk by threading them into a darning needle and taking it into the wraps.

Create a crocheted "storyteller" bag to carry your dolls and looms

(Note: It looks great with the Beanstalk Dolls stitched to it!)

Beanstalk Mesh Bag

You Will Need:

3 balls of Lily Sugar 'N Cream in your choice of colors "H" (5 mm) crochet hook

Gauge: 7 sc and 7 rows = 2 inches

Base:

Ch 8, 1 sc in 2nd ch from hook and in each remaining ch. (7 sc) ch 1, turn.

Next Row: 1 sc in each sc, ch 1 & turn (7 sc).

Repeat this row 35 times for a total of 36 rows.

Sides:

R 1: Ch 3, (counts as first dc), 1 dc in end of each row across the side edge of the base, 1 dc in each of 7 starting ch; 1 dc in end of each row along other side; 1 dc in each of 7 sc; join to top of ch 3. (86 dc).

R 2: 1 dc in each dc (86 dc).

R 3: Ch 4(counts as first dc + ch 1 space); *dc in next dc, ch 1 skip next dc*, repeat from * to * 41 times.

(43 ch 1 spaces) join to 3rd ch of the starting ch 4.

R 4 - 14: dc in next dc, ch 1 repeat around. Join to ch 3 of the starting ch 4.

R 15: *dc in ch 1, dc in next dc* from * to * to end of round.

Handle:

Ch 3 (this counts as the first dc); 1 dc in next 6 dc, (7 dc) ch 3 turn.

Repeat this row 26 times. Skip 36 dc on the top edge of bag, and join to next 7 dc across bag by sl st the 7 stitches of the handle to the next 7 dc of the bag.

Finishing the Edges of the Bag:

Ch 1, work 2 sc in the side of each dc of the handle and 1 sc of each dc of the top edge of the bag.

Sl st across the inside of the handle and repeat the sc around the other side of the handle and top of bag.

Join last sc to first sc of round, cut yarn, pull end through loop on hook then weave end into the edge stitches.

Optional: Stitch or glue a set of the Beanstalk Dolls to the bag.

Stage
pattern

The End

Meeting in the middle is a beautiful metaphor for connecting heart to heart, mind to mind, soul to soul. It has been a great joy for me to be able to meet Elinor (a truly magical soul who is a great gift to this planet), and the other wonderful people who have helped this book come to life. And now, my friend, this book is offered to you, may it come to life in your heart and hands. And, here is to meeting in the middle!

Storytelling
with Dolls

elinor peace bailey   noreen crone-findlay

How We Met in the Middle

I have been telling stories, and making dolls to tell them, for over 25 years. I am a sister to the old crones who have been spinning out the old, tattered tales that link dolls and the word for generations. We – my sisters and I – have probably carried these impulses from childhood, something I realized while watching my three-year-old grandson making story-telling magic with his own fingers. Wiggle, wiggle they go, as one finger says this and another finger says that … and this play can go on for hours.

Now, if you have an obsession, you are bound to be on the lookout for others who share it, for it is in the sharing that the most robust flavors and colors develop. That will explain why, when I saw Noreen Crone-Findlay's book, *Soul Mate Dolls*, I was curious. I snuck through the pages, peeking around corners, admiring the drawings, and wishing I had been so clever; you know how you do … like a cat rubbing the leg of a visitor, investigating a stranger. Noreen's book so struck me I found myself thinking that I should get in touch with this lady … and just like wish precedes action, an e-mail from this very author appeared on my computer, complete with an "I don't suppose you know who I am" sort of introduction!

Well, e-mail is not swift enough for me, so I called her and we tumbled about in a sea of ideas like two silly little girls. "Ah," said we, "consider the possibilities." It wasn't long before we had plans to meet and, of course, plans to perform. This idea and that idea struggled to assert itself, and then *this* one, the one about telling stories with our dolls, emerged. We had both been doing it for years and it was the strongest and the best idea of them all. Two women capturing a tale, digging into it for meaning and measure, and then spinning it out … one tale told this way, the other told that … until they meet in the middle.

It's not every day

you meet a

Noreen Crone-Findlay
dolls and puppets

A Condensed History of Dolls and Their Power

No record exists of the first time humans discovered that we could give life to our own ideas by projecting them into an inanimate object, which possessed the appearance of a human or animal. We do know that puppetry has ancient roots in the Far East, and in the Western world in Greece and Rome. From the East, it traveled throughout Asia and finally to the northwest coast of America, and from Rome and Greece it made its way through Europe. Even when the theater was rooted out of the early Christian church, a strand of it remained in puppet performances of the nativity.

In 1524, puppeteers were reported to have traveled with Cortez into Mexico, and a woman named Lenore Godomar brought puppets to Peru in 1600. The term "marionette," or little Mary, came in use in the 1800s, and by the early part of that century, children were being entertained in both France and England with puppet shows in the parks. But it is the *idea* of letting a doll form take a message to an audience that fascinates Noreen and me, no matter when that really started happening.

Let me tell you a little story about the power of dolls and their ability to bear our messages. In one of the doll-making classes that I taught, I had a student. Tall and possessing a strong voice, she was a professional kindergarten teacher in a local district. English was a second language for many of her young students, she said, and told me that her current class was learning how to count. One, two, three, four apples. How many apples do you have? Four. One of the little girls simply could not seem to grasp the concept. One day, the teacher was using a pop-up puppet in class, and the little girl became entranced. When the teacher told the class that she was going to retire the puppet for the day, the little girl begged and pleaded to let it remain. "I will stay and talk to you," said the teacher through the puppet, "If you will count for me and tell me how many apples you have." And the child proceeded to do just as the puppet asked. Although the tall, Anglo woman with the big voice had intimidated the girl, she was captivated by the smaller projection – and she was able to learn. That's amazing, isn't it? Talking through our dolls is precisely what Noreen and I propose to do in our own different ways with you.

What's So Important about Jack's Story?

From the very first, the story I chose was "Jack and the Beanstalk." Why? Because years ago, another storyteller and doll maker, Jean Ray Laury, caught my fancy by focusing her telling of this ancient tale on the throwing of the beans. You see, she said, if the Mother – the skeptic, the guardian of what we have – had not seen the beans as worthless and tossed them out the window, there would have been no beanstalk. If there had been no beanstalk then Jack, "the rash and foolish," would never have discovered the path leading to the solution of the problem. And what was the problem? Well, it was poverty, or the fear of poverty. Their poverty is embodied in the giant looming large, who, like our fear of a real or imagined crisis, eats into our consciousness like a marauding monster, keeping us from our bliss. The Hen that laid the golden eggs, in this case, represents the bliss. I was so taken by the insight Jean's interpretation gave me that I persuaded Noreen to follow the story further and play that wonderful game of "what would happen IF." As we tossed the story back and forth, like a ball over the net, and I got to walk around in it more, I could see the dolls I would use to perform it and what I would do with them.

Jean Ray's telling of the story also made me think of myself as a Bean Thrower. Noreen is a Bean Thrower, too; we have shared the experience of taking ideas (we have many of them), and throwing them out the window to an uncertain destiny. The process we were going through now certainly involved a few, random beans. Sometimes they take root and become beanstalks which, when we climb them, lead to a fierce and forbidding giant. We have to wrestle, outwit, and throw that

Giant to the ground in order to get the Hen.

Mind you, one doesn't go looking for the gold. The gold only staves off the wolf at the door for a matter of days. No, sir! One looks for the *source* of the gold. Both Noreen and I are seeking the *hen* that will provide us with nourishment for all our lives long. I believe that the Hen is imagination, inspiration, light. I see it as it as representing the source. And thank goodness all those bean ideas don't produce beanstalks because we would be buried in giants!

And just so: Things seem to move along in season. There are some perfectly marvelous ideas lying on fallow, unfertilized soil just waiting for rain to fall so they can take root. It has been said that you will never get what you do not ask for. If the Mother had stuck the beans in her apron pocket or the cupboard in preparation for making some soup in the future, forget the beanstalk. So the energy to throw the beans must be there. Making it a practice to explore ideas, share dreams, and clarify them sometimes leaves them scattered about, gestating, and there's no telling how they'll come back to you.

At some point in this exchange, Noreen and I went our separate ways, each determined to find the wheels that got the story turned back to us. I was focused on Jack's tale and Noreen experimented with other stories, finally coming back to Jack because she felt strongly that this book would be best served if we explored the same ground. She will be telling you about her twists and turns. As for me? Well, I had to go on considering the remaining characters.

The Story of Jack and Bean Stalk and How I Imagined Telling It

Now, I will not assume you know this story … you could have missed it. So I'll wrap it up in a nutshell: Jack lives with his Mother, and they are very poor. When the cow dries up, Jack's mother sends him out to sell it, which he does to the first merchant he meets. This merchant offers him five beans, which he claims are magic. Jack's Mother is so angry when she hears Jack's tale that she throws the beans out the window. Overnight they sprout into a beanstalk, which reaches upward, beyond what the eye can see, to a land above.

Jack climbs the beanstalk three times. On the first climb, he learns that the land is ruled by a ruthless Giant. Jack is fed and secreted by the Giant's Wife. The giant comes home for his dinner, uttering the famous "Fee-Fi-Fo-Fum! /I smell the blood of an Englishman. /Be he alive or be he dead, /I'll grind his bones /to make my bread." The Giant's Wife tells Jack to wait until her husband falls asleep after his supper, and then escape – which he does, stealing a bag of the Giant's gold on the way out.

Jack and his Mother live on this gold for a while, and then Jack climbs the beanstalk again. He is again fed by the Wife, and again he hides and escapes, this time making away with the hen that lays golden eggs.

Jack climbs the beanstalk for the third time, and this time he is on his own. As he's hiding in the dustbin, he hears the music of the golden Harp. He cannot resist the Harp, and takes it from the table. The Harp objects to being stolen, and reports the theft to her master – "Master save me!" Jack descends the beanstalk with the Giant in hot pursuit; he cries to his Mother for an ax, which she provides; and he chops down the beanstalk, sending the Giant to his death.

Jack then marries the "Usual Princess" and lives happily ever after. I assume that Jack wrote this story. Had it been written by his Mother, it would have been very different, I'm sure.

It seems to me that all of the characters within this story could represent some aspect of ourselves participating in the creative act. What creates the environment in which a person can throw those beans? We create that environment when we make a series of dolls, masks, and paper puppets, which will help retell the story. With the dolls telling the story, we can begin a dialog.

giant with his castle in amongst the clouds. In between, I thought I'd string some cording, over which I could throw the beanstalk – which I pictured as padded and quilted fabric leaves, attached to a covered cording. Later I'll show you how I did that, but right now I am just imagining. To start, we'll need to round up those two lad-

When I started visualizing things, I could see the set being comprised of two 3-1/2 foot ladders on an eight-foot table that I can stand behind. One of the ladders is to represent the house of Jack and his Mother, and the other the house of the

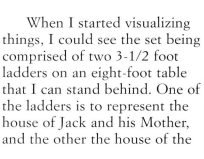

ders. As the characters in the story emerge, I will imagine them in my head, draw them in my journal, and then make them one by one, until they are all there and we're ready for that performance. Let's start with the Old Man on the Road.

Constructing the Puppets
The Old Man on the Road

Because people are very willing to believe and let their imaginations work with the performer, I have successfully used dolls as hand puppets by simply cradling them in my hand and talking through them to an audience. The dolls I have conjured up for this performance have uncomplicated button joints. They easily can be made to appear to walk … the audience will imagine the rest.

The Old Man on the Road – the trickster, the magician, the coyote who offers Jack those beans – who is he? Is he malignant, does he wish to harm Jack? The outcome suggests not, but only a madman or a trickster would offer to exchange a cow, which could at least fetch a price for her meat, for a handful of beans. Whoever he is, one could hardly prepare for him. The only

preparation is a willingness to welcome the unexpected. Can we welcome the one who sprinkles the fairy dust or sells us the short cut? What part of us believes? What part sees the possibilities? Imagination believes and sees the possibilities. Imagination turns us upside down and shows how to tweak reality. Imagination takes us places we have never dreamt of going, unveils solutions unconsidered by the rational mind. In the world of the beanstalk, the problem for Jack and his Mother is poverty, maybe even the possibility of starvation. The Mother fears she will have to beg in the street to feed her boy. In our world, poverty is perhaps a poverty of dreams, or of daring or patience. The Old Man on the Road says to us: "Forget about selling that cow for two weeks' worth of food; take these beans.

The answer is in the *beans*!"

Now the beauty of the story is that Jack – the fool, the gambler – believes. On the thin string of that belief hangs the solution that he will never be hungry again. He will make that leap of faith, the beans will prove to be magic, they will be thrown, up will pop a beanstalk, which he will climb, outsmarting the Wife of the Giant, the Giant himself, and stealing the hen and the harp and seeing to the feeding of his Mother, the wedding to a Princess and the happily ever after. But he doesn't know that yet. He only knows that he no longer has the cow, and in his pocket is a handful of beans.

Let's start with making some of the dolls we will need to tell our story. First come the patterns, followed by the instructions.

Note:

I GIVE YOU PERMISSION TO USE A COPIER TO COPY THE PATTERN PIECES FROM THIS BOOK. Check to see if there is distortion. Copy each doll's pieces and put them in separate envelopes to create some order out of the usual chaos. I will write the instructions assuming that you have copied the pieces before you begin.

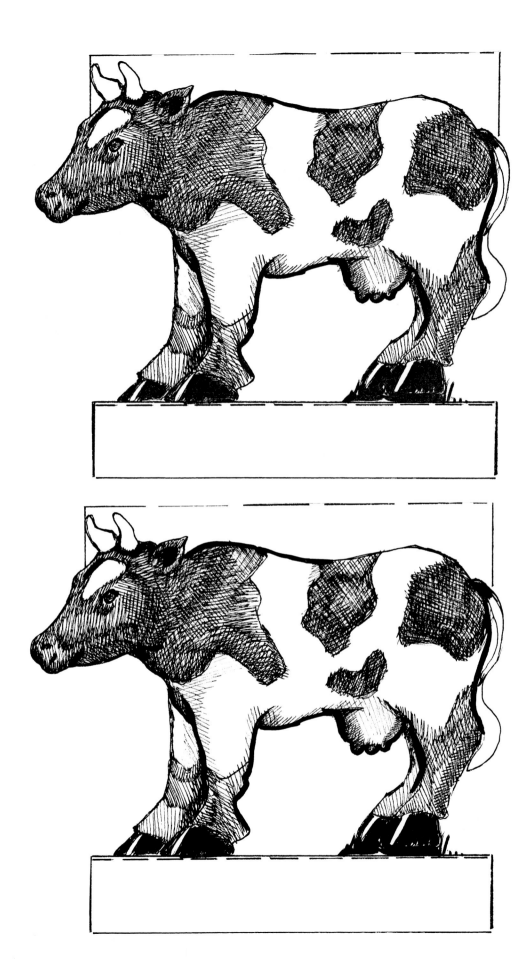

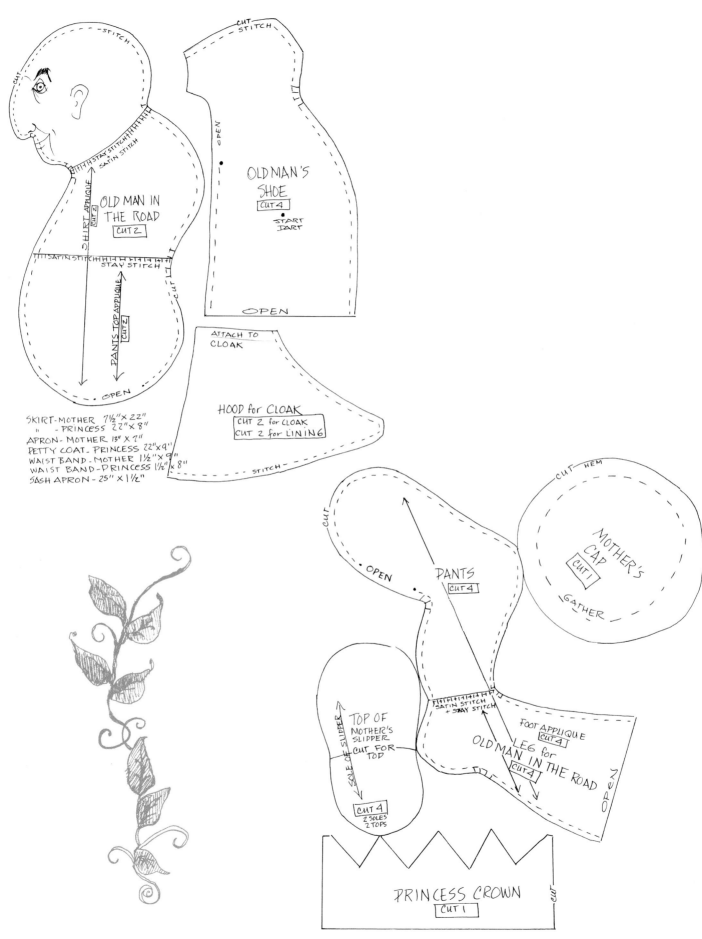

STITCH — CUT

CUT — STITCH

OLD MAN IN THE ROAD
CUT 2

SHIRT APPLIQUE CUT 2

STAY STITCH
SATIN STITCH

SATIN STITCH
STAY STITCH

PANTS TOP APPLIQUE CUT 2

• OPEN

OPEN

OLD MAN'S SHOE
CUT 4

START DART

OPEN

ATTACH TO CLOAK

HOOD for CLOAK
CUT 2 for CLOAK
CUT 2 for LINING

STITCH

SKIRT - MOTHER 7½" X 22"
"   - PRINCESS 22" X 8"
APRON - MOTHER 13" X 7"
PETTY COAT - PRINCESS 22" X 9"
WAIST BAND - MOTHER 1½" X 9"
WAIST BAND - PRINCESS 1½" X 8"
SASH APRON - 25" X 1½"

CUT

• OPEN

PANTS
CUT 4

CUT HEM

MOTHER'S CAP
CUT 1

GATHER

TOP OF MOTHER'S SLIPPER
CUT FOR TOP

SOLE OF SLIPPER

SATIN STITCH + STAY STITCH

FOOT APPLIQUE
CUT 4

LEG for OLD MAN IN THE ROAD
CUT 4

OPEN

CUT 4
2 SOLES
2 TOPS

PRINCESS CROWN
CUT 1

CUT

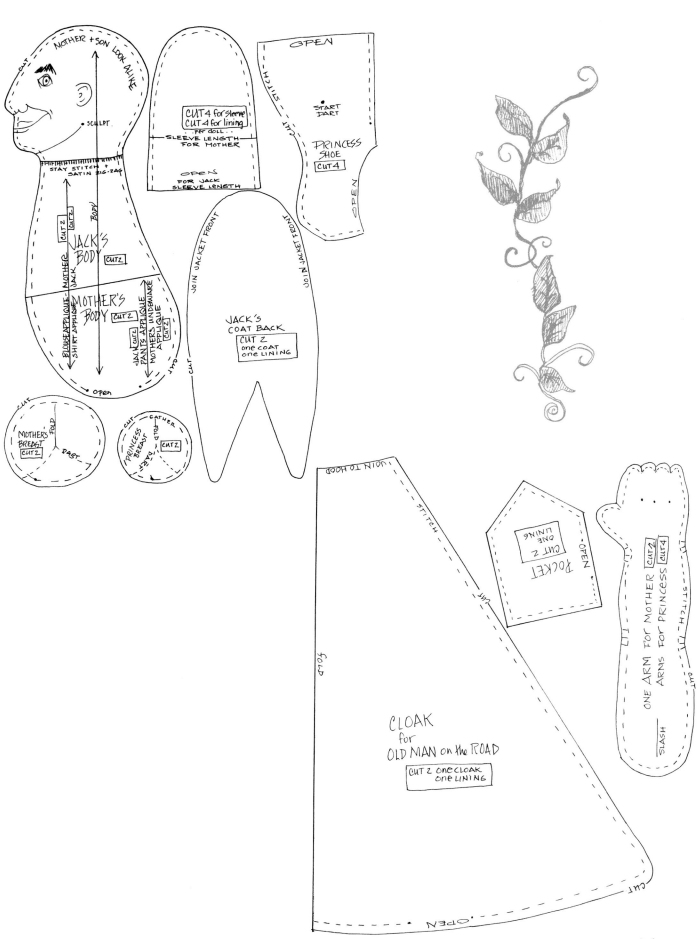

MOTHER + SON LOOK ALIKE

CUT

SCULPT.

STAY STITCH +
SATIN ZIG-ZAG

BODY

CUT 2

CUT 2

JACK'S
BODY

CUT 2

BLOUSE APPLIQUE → MOTHER
SHIRT APPLIQUE → JACK

MOTHER'S
BODY

CUT 2

PANTS APPLIQUE ← JACK CUT 2
UNDERWARE APPLIQUE ← MOTHER'S CUT 2

CUT

open

CUT

MOTHER'S
BREAST
CUT 2

FOLD

DART

CUT
GATHER

PRINCESS
BREAST

FOLD

DART

CUT 2

CUT 4 for Sleeve
CUT 4 for lining
· per doll ·
SLEEVE LENGTH
FOR MOTHER

OPEN

OPEN
FOR JACK
SLEEVE LENGTH

JOIN JACKET FRONT

JOIN JACKET FRONT

JACK'S
COAT BACK

CUT 2
one COAT
one LINING

CUT

OPEN

STITCH

CUT

START
DART

PRINCESS
SHOE
CUT 4

OPEN

OPEN

JOIN TO HOOD

STITCH

CUT

FOLD

CLOAK
for
OLD MAN on the ROAD

CUT 2 one CLOAK
one LINING

OPEN

CUT

POCKET
CUT 2
ONE
LINING

OPEN

LIT

ONE ARM FOR MOTHER CUT 2
ARMS FOR PRINCESS CUT 4

STITCH

CUT

SLASH

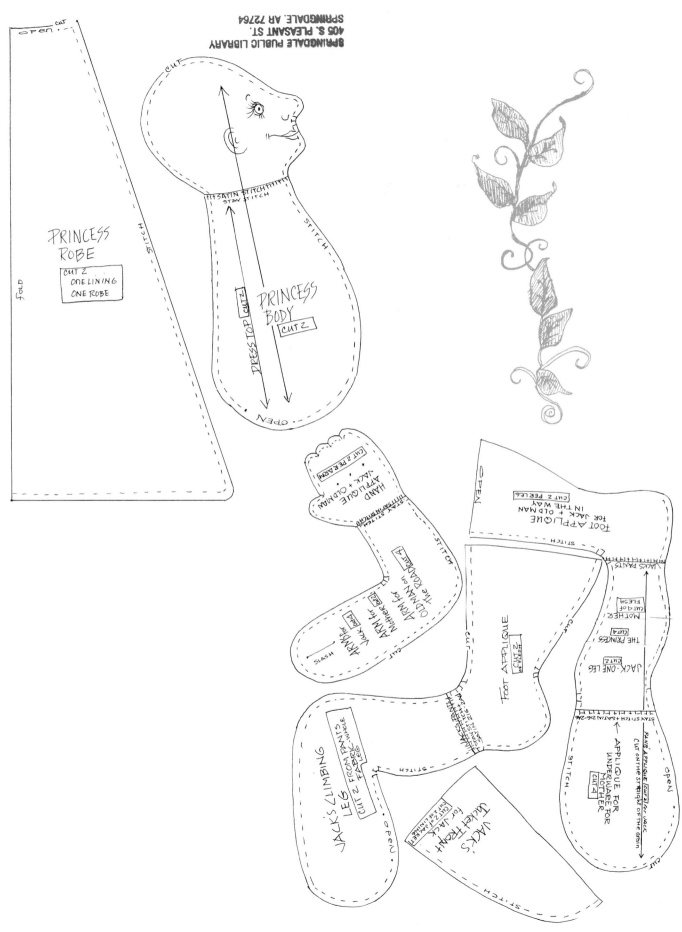

PRINCESS
ROBE

CUT 2
ONE LINING
ONE ROBE

FOLD

STITCH

CUT

OPEN

PRINCESS
BODY

CUT 2

DRESS TOP CUT 2

SATIN STITCH
STAY STITCH

STITCH

OPEN

CUT

STAY STITCH

CUT 2 PER ARM

HAND
APPLIQUE
JACK + OLD MAN

ARM for
the OLD MAN

ARM for
Mother JACK

ARM for
Jack

SLASH

STITCH

JACK'S CLIMBING
LEG FROM PANTS
CUT 2 FROM FABRIC - WHOLE
LEG

JACK'S PANTS
STAY STITCH +2 16-246

OPEN

FOOT APPLIQUE
CUT 2

FOOT APPLIQUE
FOR JACK + OLD MAN
IN THE WAY
CUT 2 PER LEG

OPEN

JACK'S PANTS

MOTHER
CUT 4 OF
FLESH

THE PRINCESS
CUT 2

JACK-ONE LEG
CUT 2

STAY STITCH + SATIN 2/6-246

APPLIQUE FOR
UNDERWARE FOR
MOTHER
CUT 4

PANTS & APPLIQUE CUT 2 for JACK

CUT ON THE STRAIGHT OF THE GRAIN

STITCH

OPEN

JACK'S
JACKET FRONT
for JACK
CUT 2 & 1 PLACE
CUT 2 OF LINING

STITCH

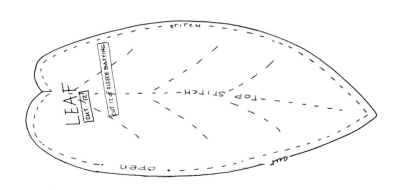

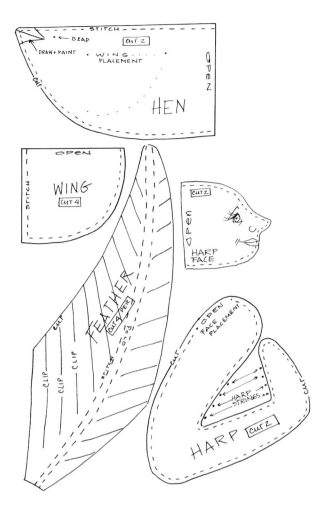

STITCH

← BEAD

CUT 2

DRAW + PAINT

WING PLACEMENT

OPEN

CUT

HEN

OPEN

WING

STITCH

CUT 4

CUT 2

OPEN

HARP FACE

FEATHER

CUT 4 PER

CUT

CUT

CLIP

CLIP

CLIP

SEAMS TO FOLD

OPEN

FACE PLACEMENT

CUT

CUT

HARP STRINGS

HARP

CUT 2

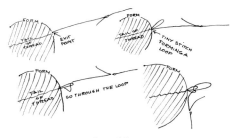

ladder stitch

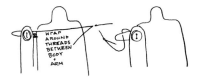

colonial knot

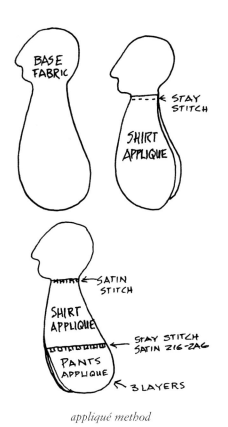

sheep shank

appliqué method

Stitches Used for Basic Doll-Making

Basic doll making stitches include: the *Ladder stitch* (see diagram at left); *Colonial knot* or anchoring stitch is created by entering the needle far away enough to create a tail inside the doll about 1-1/2". Do not use a knot on the end of your thread. Exit the needle where you wish the knot to be. Make a tiny stitch; this will form a loop. Bring the needle through the loop from the back and weave the needle under the thread as it comes from the doll. This should form a figure 8. Pull slowly and this creates your anchoring stitch:

Sheep shank. This is done as part of joining the limbs to the body. It is the stitch that helps to form a shank of the threads after the limb is joined. Wrap the thread around the threads between the limb and the body. Pull. Catch one wrap on your finger and bring the needle through that loop. Pull. Repeat this and form a colonial knot to anchor.

Bury the thread.

I use an *Appliqué Method* for dressing my dolls. First, I select a base fabric. In the case of the Old Man's Leg, I chose to make the pants the base fabric. I cut the whole leg from the pants fabric. I cut out the foot from the fabric I had selected for the flesh of the Old Man, using the pattern piece on the leg marked foot appliqué. I lay that on top of the pants fabric where the foot is intended to be. Then I sew it up and the leg appears to be clothed. All the instructions to appliqué one surface onto another require that you use a stay stitch or straight stitch, on the exposed raw edge, first to hold the appliqué in place. Then, you cover the raw edge with a satin zigzag stitch. The satin zigzag stitch is not a structural stitch and will not hold the fabric together.

The *template method* may be called for. It means that you trace the pattern piece and use it as a template. Draw around it on your selected fabric with right sides together. Stitch slightly within the lines, then cut out the piece. Leave a generous 1/8" seam allowance.

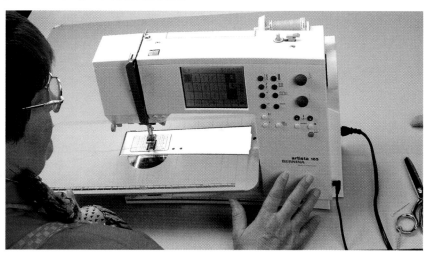

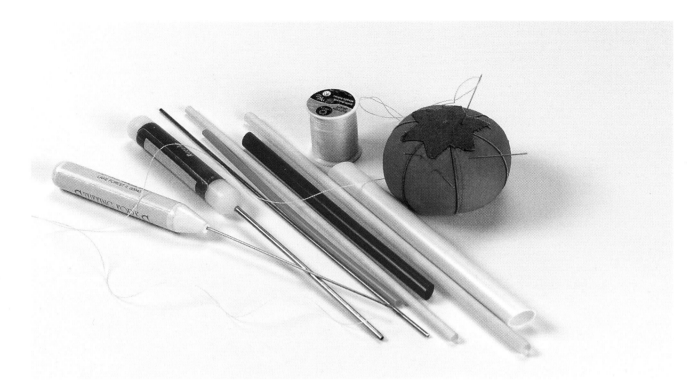

General Tools

Woven Cotton, 100% — is the most predictable fabric to use for making dolls. This is what I recommend if you are a beginner. I use it to design doll bodies because my strong suit is drawing, and the woven cotton holds drawing lines. If you choose to use blends or other more exotic fabrics such as silk, ultra-suede or a knit, I assume you can handle the problems they may present. Lamé must be backed with a knit, iron-on interfacing. It is not very durable.

Turn-It-All — a turning tool designed by Specialty Distributors (previously known as the "Bow Whip").

Stuffing Fork — (standard, and small sizes), designed by Barbara Willis. You may wish to include a hemostat. Get the Turn-It-All and the Stuffing Fork at your local quilt shop or order them from epb. Wooden spoons and other makeshift tools are usually not as successful as those that have been developed for the task.

#7 Long Darner — by John James of Piecemakers, is used for putting the dolls together and sculpting the faces.

3" Doll Makers' Needle — for assembling the dolls. Available through epb.

Poly-fil by Fairfield Processing — What you select for stuffing dolls makes a big difference. I recommend this brand. You may wish to experiment and find out which stuffing meets your needs. If you stuff with a long-fibered garneted stuffing (which gives you a hard pack), you will have more success stuffing with very small pieces. The usual rule is "small pieces in small places and large pieces in large places," but when your stuffing is long-fibered, it comes from material prepared for quilt batting, minus the heat setting. Garneted, long-fibered stuffing tends to lump, or felt, so small pieces are always best. Tear this kind of stuffing apart for best results. If you are using siliconized stuffing it will be very slippery and a bit hard to get a hold of and pack. When you succeed the pack is smooth. But the experience may be frustrating. Poly-fil by Fairfield is made with a different process, which explodes the fiber at cross-purposes. The fiber is short and smooth, and therefore harder to felt in the casing. I prefer a very firm, but not hard, pack so this works for me. Here the rule applies about the size and placement of the pieces. Do, however, get the pieces (whatever the size), *where* they belong … don't pave the road with good intentions. The fabric that you select to make your doll will also affect the stuffing. A blend of cotton and poly will make stuffing a challenge. Silk needs a gentle touch; velours and knits will hide a multitude of stuffing sins but distort the line and make painting a face very difficult. When stuffing larger pieces, you can line the casing with a fleece batting and create a smooth stuff – experience will teach you many tricks.

Coats and Clark® Dual Duty, Button, Carpet, and Craft thread — for joining the limbs and sculpting the faces of the dolls.

Prym Dritz "Fray-Check" — is indispensable in checking the fraying on small seams and at points of clipping. Turn the pieces before they dry.

.03 Permawriter II in brown by Y&C (Yasutomo & CO) — to paint the faces of the dolls.

FabricMate pens by Y&C — for drawing in face features.

Any white fabric paint and/or Crayola Crayons — for color and shading. A starter kit is available through epb.

Sewing Machine — Your sewing machine should be your best friend. Clean and check it often. Every eight hours of sewing you should change your needle. I use a Universal #12 by Schmetz and a scant 1/4" to 1/8" seam allowance. Do not use cheap thread. It will wreak havoc with your machine and its tension. Any thread on a *wooden* spool is too old.

Notes:

Always be in the process of collecting doll-scale prints, bits, and pieces. They will lend spark to your dolls.

To avoid losing your pattern pieces, use envelopes to store them after you have copied and cut them out. A piece of foam core board next to your work station can be used to pin the pieces you are working on or have sewn so that you will not spend all your sewing time looking for them.

The Old Man in the Road

This is what you'll need to make the Old Man. I have constructed the Old Man, Jack, his Mother, and the Usual Princess the same way. Only the drawings are changed, so there will be references to this first pattern in the remaining three. These are peasant people, and so I have given them very large feet and rather homely faces (I hope the peasants among you will not be too insulted). They are all of a family and so they resemble each other, except the Princess: She gets to be pretty. When the directions for one doll apply to the making of another, we may refer you to the first pattern, thus making you a little crazy and giving us some additional space. When one doll differs from the other in some detail, those will be included with the pattern to which they apply.

Instructions for Making the Old Man

To construct the Old Man's body:

1 Trace of the appliqué patterns for the foot, hand, shirt, and top of pants. Take note of the arrow, which will tell you where the appliqué pattern begins and ends.

2 Cut the pieces for the body and appliqués for shirt and top of pants from selected fabric. Stack the appliqué on the body, which is the base fabric, and stay-stitch them in place. Cover the raw edges that will not be caught in the seam with a satin zigzag stitch.

3 Place some Poly-fil at the side of the nose next to the stitch plate so that it will flip into the seam. Stitch the body, right sides together, leaving open where indicated on the pattern piece. Clip, turn, and stuff firmly. Close, by hand, using a ladder stitch. Set aside.

Materials for making the Old Man in the Road:

Along with your general supplies and tools you will need:

Scraps of woven cotton for his flesh (he is weather beaten), for his pants, shirt, and the bag for the beans

1/4 yd for his cloak and its lining

A scrap of felt for his shoes.

4 buttons for his joints, 2 buttons for his shoes

Loose goat hair for his hair and beard. If you can only find white, dye it

A walking stick and a bit of string for the bag

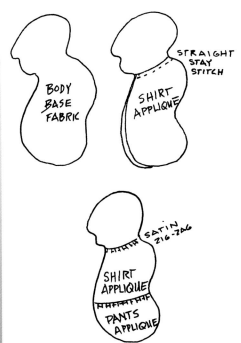

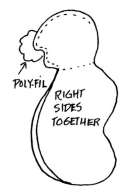

To construct the Old Man's arms and legs:

1. Trace the appliqué for the foot and hand from the paper pattern.

2. The base fabric for the leg will be the pants, and the base fabric for the arms will be the sleeve. Lay the appliqués on the base fabric and stay-stitch them in place. Cover the raw edge with a satin zigzag stitch.

3. With right sides together, stitch the legs and the arms; leave open when indicated on the pattern pieces. Leave the arm open on the fat seam at the upper arm.

4. Press the two seams together at the toe. Stitch an arc across the seams to form the foot. Clip, turn, and stuff firmly. Close by hand with the ladder stitch and set aside.

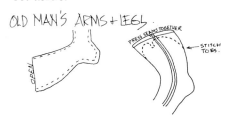

Sculpting the Old Man's Face:

This process will be used in all four doll patterns.

1. Using a #7 long darner and Button, Carpet, and Craft thread with no knot, bring the needle into the back of the head and exit to #1 at the tear duct. Form a colonial knot on the surface. Re-enter at #1, a few threads away and exit at the second tear duct, #2. Re-enter at #2, a few threads away, and exit back at #1, pulling slightly, to achieve an indentation. Repeat this until the thread holds this indentation between the two tear ducts. This is the placement for the corner of the eye. Re-enter at #2 and exit at the hole of the first nostril, #3. Re-enter at #3 and exit at #2, pull. Reenter at #2 and exit at #1. Re-enter at #1 and exit at the second nostril hole #4. Reenter at #4 and exit at #1. Pull. Re-enter at #1 and exit at #5, the other corner of the eye. Re-enter at #5 and exit at #6. Re-enter at #6 and exit at #5. Pull to form the cheek or smile. Re-enter at #5 and exit at #6. Wrap the thread to #7 to crease the mouth and enter at #7 and exit at #8. Pull. (Are you confused yet? It gets worse.) Re-enter at #8 and exit at #7. Re-enter at #7 and exit at #8 and go to #9 where we will form the chin. Wrap the thread to #10. Enter at #10 and return under the surface to #9. Make another colonial knot to tie off and bury the thread emerging wherever. At the end of this ordeal, shout into the air and carry on, in a natural expression of triumph.

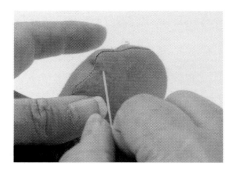

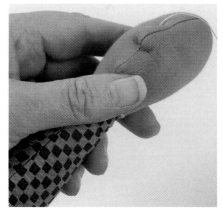

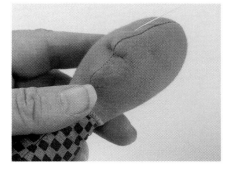

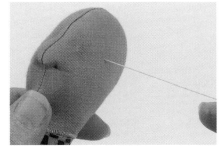

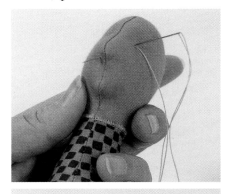

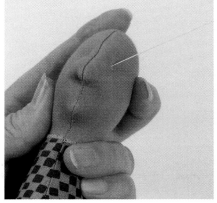

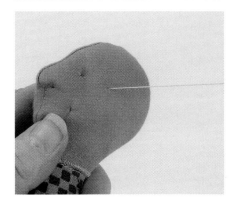

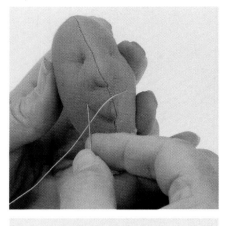

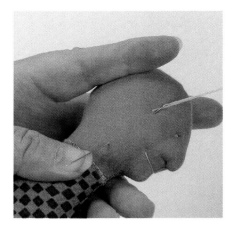

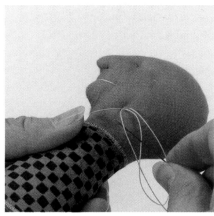

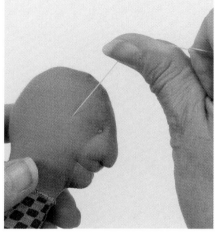

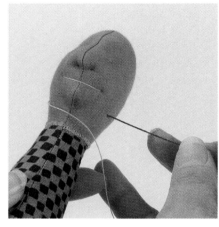

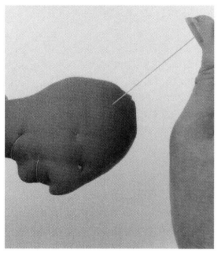

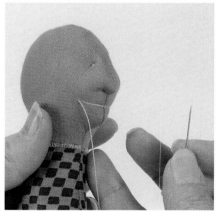

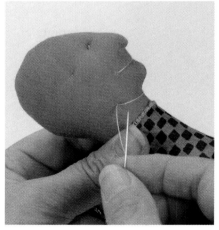

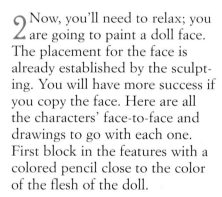

2 Now, you'll need to relax; you are going to paint a doll face. The placement for the face is already established by the sculpting. You will have more success if you copy the face. Here are all the characters' face-to-face and drawings to go with each one. First block in the features with a colored pencil close to the color of the flesh of the doll.

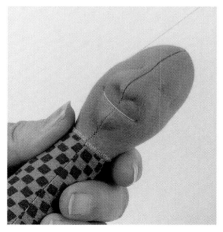

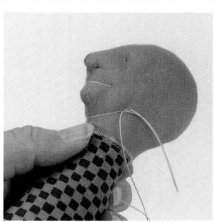

3 Next, draw in the features with a fine tipped permanent marking pen.

4 Use the fabric brush tipped pens for the bold color and the Crayola crayon for the softer color and shading. Finally, paint the whites of the eyes with the white fabric paint and add highlight to the eye a little over the pupil.

Sculpting the Old Man's feet:
Use your #7 long darner and Button, Carpet, and Craft thread. Do not knot the thread. Mark the foot with a pencil to indicate the placement of the toes. Bring the needle from the heel to between the large toe and the remaining toes at #1. Take a tiny stitch and form a colonial knot on the surface to anchor the stitch. Over cast the thread to the bottom of

the foot and enter at #2. Exit at #1 and pull to form the first toe. Re-enter at #1 and exit at #2. Pull to secure. Re-enter at #2 and exit at #3, pulling again. Re-enter at #3 and overcast to #4 at the back of the foot and repeat this until you have formed five toes; you must count them, or you could be counted among long list of people who have given their doll six toes. When you complete the

fifth toe and you have returned to #8,
re-enter at #8 and exit at #9 to form the arch of the foot. Overcast the thread to #10 and exit at #9. Re-enter at #9 and exit at #10. Pull. Re-enter at #10 and exit at #11. Overcast the thread to #12 to form the ankle. Re-enter at #12 and exit at #11. Pull and make a tiny stitch form the colonial knot. Bury the thread and exit wherever.

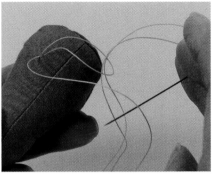
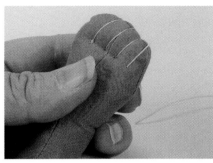

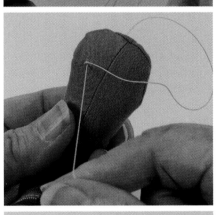
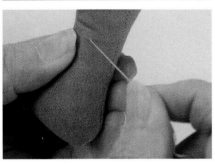

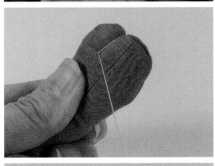
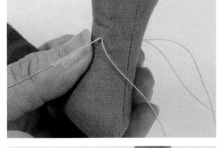

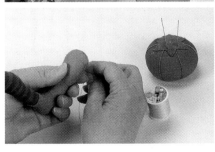
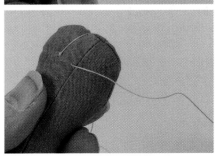
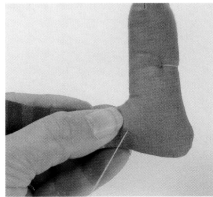

Sculpting the Old Man's hands:
Use your #7 long darner and Button, Carpet, and Craft thread. Do not knot the thread. Mark the hand with a pencil to indicate the placement of the four fingers. The thumb is independent already. Bring the needle from the wrist to #1.

Overcast the thread to #2. Enter at #2 and exit at #1. Pull. Re-enter at #1 and exit at #2. Pull. Re-enter at #2 and exit at #3. Pull again and overcast to #4. Re-enter at #4 and exit at #3. Re-enter at #3 and exit at #4. Re-enter at #4 and exit at #5. Pull again and Overcast to #6.

Enter at #6 and exit at #5. Re-enter at #5 and exit at #6. Pull. Re-enter at #6 and exit at #7 at the wrist. Re-enter at #7 and exit at #8 in the palm. Re-enter at #8 and exit at #7. Pull and anchor the thread by forming a colonial knot. Bury the thread and exit wherever.

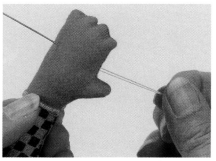

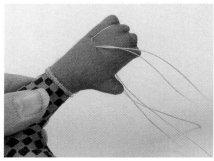

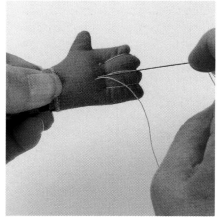

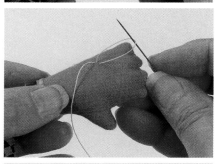

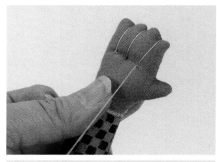

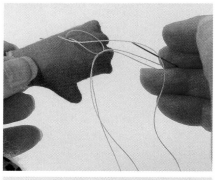

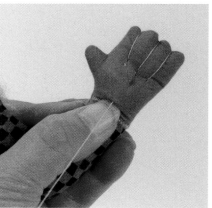

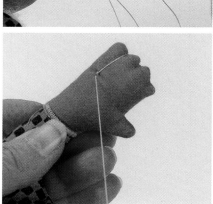

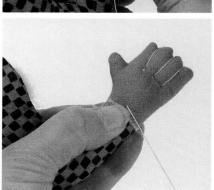

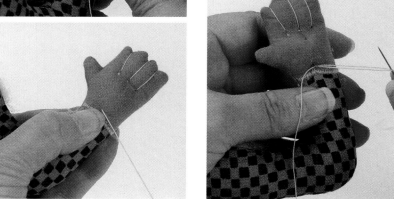

Assembling the Old Man's body:

To assemble the body, use a 3" doll maker's needle and Button, Carpet, and Craft thread. Place the knot between the arm and the body. If the arm has a cap sleeve, place it on the top of the arm. Bring the needle through the arm from the back and string on the button from its backside. Bring the needle through the button again and into the arm, then into the body. If the body has a coat over it, put it on for this process. Return to the outside of the button to secure. Return through the button to the other side of the body and string on the remaining arm and button. Return to the other sides. Pass through the second button three times to secure, and the wrap the thread around the threads between the arm and the body three times. Form a loop, wrapping it over your finger, and bring the needle through. Pull to secure, and hold out another loop, bringing the needle through. Pull again and tie off with a colonial knot. Bury the thread and exit where ever you choose. Clip. The same process will attach the legs.

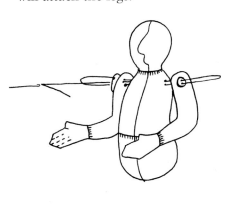

To make shoes for the Old Man's feet:

1 Cut the shoes from the felt scraps. Press the two seams together at the toe. Stitch a graduated point to the toe, starting where the pattern piece indicates.

OLD MAN'S SHOES

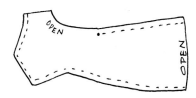

2 Trim off the excess fabric and turn. Fold over the point where the toes will be, and secure the tip of the point to the shoe with a button.

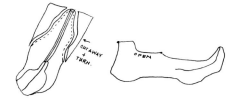

To make the Old Man's cloak:

1 Cut the cloak, the hood and the cloak and hood lining from selected fabric. With right sides together, stitch the hood and the hood lining where indicated on the pattern piece. With right sides together, join the hood to the cloak and the hood lining to the cloak lining at the neck where indicated on the paper pattern.

OLD MAN'S CLOAK

2 With right sides together, stitch the lining to the cloak at all the raw edges. Leave an opening at the bottom to turn. Turn and press. Close the opening by hand.

To make the Old Man's bag:

1 Cut the scrap of fabric for the bag 3" x 4". Fold, with right sides together width wise and stitch on three sides. Turn. Fold down the raw edge into the bag and press in a hem to form a casing. Stitch, leaving a small opening through which to lead the string.

2 Lead the string through with a safety pin. Knot each end of the string and tie it onto the arm of the Old Man. This is where the beans go. (Oh, boy! Read: "Trip to the grocery store to get a bag of kidney beans and a nice cold drink.") Put the beans in the bag with some fairy dust.

To make the Old Man's hair and beard:

There is sometimes available at craft stores loose goat hair, but it is intended for Santa hair and so it is white. You can dye it with hair dye or Rit™ dye. Make the hair gray. Form tiny clumps and stitch one onto the top of his head and a bit on his chin for a goatee. Find him a gnarled stick for his walking stick and sew it into his hand. With a little luck the Old Man stands. Put him on the road.

Jack

Within many of us, there is a daredevil … that part of us who jumps into the boiling pot and never sees the consequences … who has the vision but does not count the cost … a risk taker who acts first and thinks afterward. Without the spontaneity of this inner child, life would be very dull. We would build no castles in the sky without foundation, and life would yield few surprises but, it must be said, we might all be a lot *safer*. Still, the Jack in us needs free reign. Let's call his function "play." The playful manipulation of words, whether material or tonal, is at the center of the creative act. But after the play, there is production which requires self-governance, and that is in the domain of the Mother. What we are seeking here is balance.

As we mature, we learn not to act on an impulse without giving it close examination. Of course, some of us learn this lesson *too* well and too *soon*. We live cautiously when daring might be called for. We perceive danger where none exists, and we find consequences dire when the choices we make simply don't matter to anyone but ourselves. Nowhere is this more the case than in our artistic and creative lives. Choices about color and shape and size loom large. We allow rules to be piled around us, forming a wall to keep us safe. We ask ourselves to what degree will we be exposed, or what will our sisters, teachers, or our best friends think? Chances are these fearful thoughts were instilled in us early, and they probably will never leave. Like Jack, then, we must find a way to be creatively nimble and quick, and jump over the candlestick of our own anxiety.

Instructions for Making Jack

Jack's body

1 Trace the appliqué patterns for the foot, hand, shirt, and top of pants. Take note of the arrow, which will tell you where the appliqué pattern begins and ends.

2 Cut the pieces for the body and appliqués for shirt and top of pants from selected fabric. Stack the appliqué on the body, which is the base fabric, and stay-stitch them in place. Cover the raw edges that will not be caught in the seam with a satin zigzag stitch.

3 Place some poly-fil at the side of the nose next to the stitch plate, so that it will flip into the seam. With right sides together, stitch the body, leaving open where indicated. Clip, turn, and stuff firmly. Close, by hand, using a ladder stitch. Set aside.

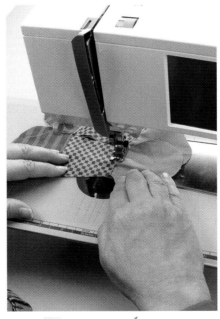

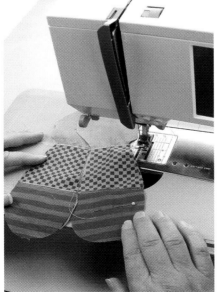

To make Jack's arms and legs:

1 Trace the appliqué for the foot and hand from the paper pattern.

2 The base fabric for the leg will be the pants, and the base fabric for the arms will be the sleeve. Lay the appliqués on the base fabric and stay-stitch them in place. Cover the raw edge with a satin zigzag stitch.

3 With right sides together, stitch the legs and the arms; leave open when indicated.

4 There will be two openings on the foot. Press the seams together at the toe and make an arched stitch line to form the toe. Trim the excess fabric. Clip, turn, and stuff firmly.

5 Open the arm with a 1/2" slash through one layer at the top where indicated on the pattern piece. Clip, turn, and stuff firmly.

See pages 60-63 for directions to sculpt the face, hands, and feet.

See page 61 for instructions about painting Jack's face.

To make the swallow-tailed coat and sleeve for Jack:

1 Cut out the jacket, sleeves, and linings from selected fabric.

2 With right sides together, stitch the two front pieces of the jacket to the back. Do the same with the long pieces. The sleeves are separate and will fit over the arms.

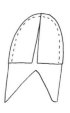

JACKET

3 With right sides together, stitch the body of the jacket to the body of the lining. Leave open to turn. Clip, turn, and press. Close the opening by hand.

4 Sleeves. Pay attention – this is tricky. Cut out four sleeves for the lining and four for the jacket. Stitch the sleeves in pairs with right sides together, matching sleeves with sleeves and lining with lining.

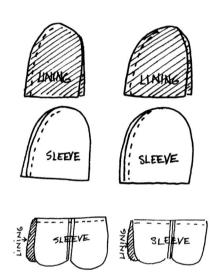

5 Press the seams open. With right sides together, stitch the pairs of lining to the pairs of the jacket on the flat side. Press.

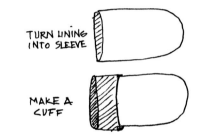

6 Fold each unit lengthwise and, with right sides together, stitch around the outer edge. Leave an opening on the line to turn. Turn and stuff the lining into the sleeve. Slip over the arm before joining the arm to the body and slip the jacket across Jack's shoulders as well.

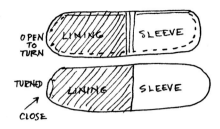

See page 64 for directions to assemble Jack's arms and legs.

To make the hat and hair for Jack:

1 Use small clumps of loose goat hair, which you have dyed to suit. Stitch them in place. Jack has a fair amount of hair that he will lose in about 15 years. Some things never change.

2 Use the hat pattern to cut Jack's hat from your scrap of felt. Stitch them and turn the hat. Pull it over Jack's head. Perhaps a bit of a cuff would be nice … he will tell you. Stitch it in place. And now to the Cow.

Materials for making the cow:

The cow copied from page 49
A small cardboard box, at least 4-1/2" x 3-1/2" and 1-1/2" deep for the cow to ride on
A pad of watercolor paper
A paper gluestick and craft glue
1/2 yd of string
Two 1/4" wooden dowels a little wider than the width of your box
A utility knife and an awl

Instructions for Making the Cow

1 Photocopy the cows on page 49 and cut them out.

2 Mount them on the watercolor paper with the paper glue stick and cut them out with the utility knife. To protect your cutting surface, place a piece of cardboard underneath.

3 Score the centerfold (that is, cut without cutting through), and also the line under the feet of the cow. This will create the stand.

4 Using the utility knife, make four notches this size. Two on each side of the box to hold the dowel axel.

5 Trace the pattern for the wheels and cut them out from the watercolor paper using the utility knife. Use the awl to punch holes in the center of each wheel and fix each wheel to an end of the two dowels with the craft glue. This will fit into the notches you have made in the box.

6 Affix the cow to the box with the craft glue on the hinged stand. Make a hole at the front of the box to put the string through. Fold the string in half and put the loop through the hole. Bring the other end through the loop and pull. Now Jack can lead that poor old Cow down the road to meet the Old Man.

Continuing with the Tale

Now, we are all standing about shaking our collective finger at Jack, warning him about his impending doom; soon he'll be off snatching that Hen and scooting down the beanstalk followed by a roaring Giant. If he'd had good sense, if he'd done what his Mother told him to do, well ... they'd be begging for food; as it is, he will bring us to the source, the imagination, and the light. However, it takes all kinds; and what would we have done without the Mother to throw those beans? I see her as the guardian, *and* the skeptic. She worries. She looks into the future and the future is bleak. If there is a strong mother inside you, such as Jack's, it is best to identify her, make her real, and assign her certain tasks.

When you make her real within you (and when you make the doll, too!), have a conversation with her. Be firm and decisive. Have her balance your checkbook, help you cross the street, help you pick a mate or consider a large purchase, but leave her at home if you are scheduled to meet an old man on the road, because she'll talk you out of the magic beans and that's for sure.

The part of you that's cautious is good, but it has its place, particularly in your creative world. In your artistic life where creativity and spontaneity are the coin of exchange, the Jack in you will be more useful. Taking chances creatively, with color and with form and texture is a playful act. It is very much a matter of letting go rather than holding on. The most creative thing that Jack's mother ever did was to let go of those beans. What an artist needs most to let go of is the perfectionism that asks her to make art without experience, because failure is the artist's chief instructor. It is far better to make bad art than not to make art at all. The Jack's Mother within you would never let you do that. She would advise you to stick to what you do well – in her case, that would mean starving, rather than risk trusting in the magic.

Funny – isn't it? – her contempt for the beans also leads her to throw them out the window where they produce the beanstalk ... the adventure. Now, we have to figure out how to make the doll of the mother do that.

Instructions for Making the Mother

Body

1 Trace of the appliqué patterns for dress and underwear top and bottom. Take note of the arrow, which will tell you where the appliqué pattern begins and ends.

2 Cut the pieces for the body and appliqués for the dress and top of underwear from selected fabric. Stack the appliqué on the body, which is the base fabric and stay stitch them in place. Cover the raw edges that will not be caught in the seam with a satin zigzag stitch.

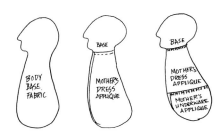

3 Put the two body pieces with right sides together. Place

some poly-fil at the side of the nose next to the stitch plate so that it will flip into the seam. Stitch the body, leaving open where indicated on the pattern piece. Clip, turn, and stuff firmly. Close, by hand, using a ladder stitch.

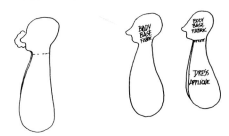

4 Cut the breast from the dress fabric. Dart them as shown below. Trim off the excess fabric and gather with matching quilting thread. Leave an opening the size of a dime at the back of the breast and stuff firmly. She is ample. Press the breast to the body, a little on the low side, and stitch in place with the ladder stitch.

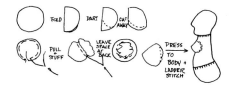

Arms and Legs

1 The base fabric for the leg will be the flesh and the arms will be the entirely the flesh. Lay the appliqué for the underwear on the leg and stay stitch in place. Cover the raw edge with a satin zigzag stitch. No lace; remember, this is a poor woman.

2 With right sides together, stitch the legs and the arms; leave open on leg where indicated to turn. Make a tiny slash (1/2"), through one layer of the arm to turn. Clip, turn, and stuff firmly. Close by hand.

Find the directions for sculpting the face, hands, and feet on pages 60-63.

Find the instructions about painting the mothers face on page 61.

Skirt and Sleeves

1 Cut the skirt 9" x 22-1/2". Fold width-wise with right sides together. Stitch, leaving an opening at the top of 1-1/2" in which to slip the doll. Press the seam and top stitch the opening. Press a rolled hem at the bottom of the skirt and stitch in place.

2 22-1/2" is a lot of bulk to fit around that doll, so gather by hand with a knotted thread. Pull the gathers to fit around her waist. Make it fit a little on the low side, she is a bit thick about the middle. Tie off the thread and stay-stitch the gathers in place.

3 Cut the waistband 1-1/2"x 7-1/2". Fit the right side of the waistband to the wrong side of the waist of the skirt. Center to center. Pin. There should be over lap. Wrap the ends of the band 3/8" to finish the ends. Stitch in place.

4 Turn the ends of the band. Press. Fold under a tiny hem at the raw edge and with wrong sides together top stitch the band at the front of the skirt. After assembling the body, place the skirt on her and hand-tack it in place.

5 For the sleeves, pay attention – this is tricky. Cut out four sleeves for the lining and four for the jacket. Stitch the sleeves in pairs with right sides together, matching sleeves with sleeves and lining with lining.

6 Press the seams open. With right sides together, stitch the

pairs of lining to the pairs of the jacket on the flat side. Press.

7 Fold each unit lengthwise and, with right sides together, stitch around the outer edge. Leave an opening on the line to turn. Turn and stuff the lining into the sleeve. Put the sleeve on top of the arm before attaching the arm to the body.

See page 64 for instructions on how to assemble the body.

Apron
1 Cut the apron 15" x 8", the sash 25" x 1-1/2" and the pocket and lining from the paper pattern.

2 With right sides together, stitch the two pocket pieces. Leave open to turn. Turn and press. Place the pocket on the apron at the right side of the front of the apron so the Mother can use it. Top stitch in place. Hem the two 8" sides and one of the 15" sides. Make the hem in the 15" side a little deeper.

3 Gather the apron to fit the doll. It should wrap slightly to the back.

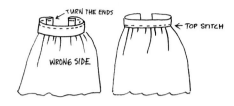

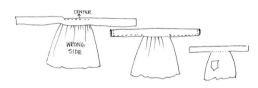

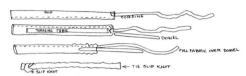

4 Fold the sash in half lengthwise. With the wrong side of the apron to the right side of the sash, center to center, pin in place, and stitch.

5 Press in a tiny hem on the raw edges of the sash and fold over the gathered edge of the apron. Top stitch. Now tie her apron on, and she is ready to serve – as serve she must.

Hair, Cap, and Slippers
1 Dye that loose goat hair a very tired shade of gray or brown. Oh dear and a sigh. Take small clumps and stitch them in place by hand.

2 To make the cap, cut it from the selected fabric and make a tiny hem around the edge. Gather to fit to her head. Tie off the gathers and tack it to her head.

3 To make the pattern for the felt slippers, place the foot bottom side down on a bit of paper. Draw around the foot. Add a "skosh" for fit. Cut the felt sole from your pattern and use the front half of the pattern for the top of the slipper. Lay the top on the sole and top stitch. Do not turn, just slip her foot in and tack in place. With a deep sigh, now, she's ready to go.

Stalking the Journey

With the throwing of the beans comes the Beanstalk. The Beanstalk represents the journey or the way. But only a fool climbs a beanstalk into the unknown, and Jack is just such a fool. Does something within us lead us to take such a chance and confront the Giant? Just like Jack's poverty, life and art present us with problems. Perhaps we are feeling impoverished, empty, or blocked. What is needed is a little carelessness.

Throw those beans without consideration of the results and climb!

The Beanstalk will be the first element of theater. I have placed my two 3-1/2 foot stepladders a couple of feet apart and created the stalk from cording. Between the ladders, I will string some monofilament. I will have to secure the ladder with duct tape and cover that with paper. This will keep the filament taut.

Instructions for Making the Beanstalk

Materials for making the Beanstalk:

45"x 2-1/2" for the stalk and another 1/4 yd for the six leaves
1/4 yd of fleece batting
1-1/4 yd of cording
Fishing line

1 Cut the six leaves, back and front from selected fabric. With right sides together, place the six paired sides on two layers of the fleece batting. Stitch. Leave open to turn. Trim excess batting and turn. Press. Close the opening by hand.

2 Quilt in the veins of the leaves by machine. This isn't hard to do; enjoy.

3 Take the 45"x 2-1/2" piece of fabric you have cut for the stem, and fold it lengthwise with right sides together. Capture one end of the cording in the end of the stem fabric. The remainder of the cording should be sticking outside the stem casing. Stitch in place, and stitch a 1/4" seam down the length of the fabric. Leave one end open. Pull the casing, right side out, over the cording. Stick the raw edge of the open end into the casing and tie a slipknot. Cut the remaining end. Push in the raw edge and tie another slipknot.

4 Two more slipknots add to the look of the thing. Stitch the leaves in place by hand down the stalk. Tie the fishing line at the top end. The leaves should hang down.

Fee Fi Fo Fum — the Confrontation

In the beginning, Jack's climb and exploration of the castle where the Giant lives is simply a boyish game. It is my experience that many problems are best addressed with game-playing. Poking about, letting solutions come and go freely. This book came about beginning with two artists at play. When we first started throwing out ideas, I saw all my puppets in doll forms. That was where I was most comfortable, but Noreen's mind is much more flexible and inventive. She suggested paper dolls for some of the characters and maybe even masks. That delighted me.

At first, we thought we might make the pieces together. She chose some and I chose others. The minute she mentioned paper, I saw my Giant looking similar to an Indonesian shadow puppet with three legs circling about like a windmill tearing after Jack. I saw him made of watercolor paper with a brad holding his legs to his body, allowing them to move. I could color him, or leave him stark white for drama. I could glue him to a stick so that I could hold him in one hand to tear after Jack, who I held in the other hand, and roaring. That ought to give Jack focus.

As we considered the scene, it occurred to me that the giant's wife might be a mask, because I could wear that and still hold onto the other characters. When she was there I would pull the mask down, and when she was not I could pull the mask back onto the top of my head. All this creative production came from the interaction between Noreen and me while we were on the telephone. It was exciting. But no matter how good the chemistry, we each had to have control over our parts of the play, and so we returned to our own search.

The wife of the Giant is an opportunist. She hates the Giant but she's terrified of him, too, and she needs him at some level to fit into her worldview, which says: "The world is a hard place and you are on your own; my own protection is my own business." She will not lay her life on the line for Jack, but she knows what's up and she'll help and watch, stand back. Without the Giant's Wife, Jack hasn't a prayer. He would be caught red-handed … so, Jack charms her into becoming his accomplice. But she will never initiate, and she only does what she *has* to do. There are times when I sell out to her. I have given a sufficiency to some project and although it isn't marvelous, it is good enough. She is the measured response. Too much of her and you are a fraud … too little, and you are exhausted or burned out. Balance in your creative life is very hard to strike. Like the poppies in the *Wizard of Oz*, your inner life can overwhelm everything else. Making a list of what you want on your tombstone may do the trick; consider these: "She Made a Lot of Stuff" *or*, "She was a great mom and grandmother and she loved well." There are choices, after all.

Materials for making the Giant and His Wife:

Watercolor pad
Colored pencil to color the Giant
Photo copies of the Giant and the mask for the Giant's Wife. You may wish to copy them a little larger. Make him as large as you like, he is your Giant
1 brass brad
Utility knife
1/4" wooden dowel 18" long
Awl and a paper glue stick
Scrap of fabric for a pocket to hold the dowel
Enough round elastic to hold the mask to your face

Instructions for Making the Giant and His Wife

1 Color the Giant with your colored pencils. Enjoy!

2 Cut both pieces out and mount them on the watercolor paper with the paper glue stick. Cut them out with the utility knife. Cut out the blacked in area on the Wife's mask. Use a piece of cardboard to protect the cutting surface.

3 Use the awl to make a hole for the brad to fit through at the Giant's navel and through the center of the running legs. Enter the brad and spring the brad.

4 Cut a 2-1/2" square of fabric from the fabric scrap. Fold it lengthwise and stitch up two sides. Turn. Use craft glue to stick one side to the head of the Giant, creating a pocket for the dowel. OOOH … scary!

5 Tie the elastic in place at the side of the Wife's mask. Fit it to your face.

The Usual Princess

The Usual Princess is the reward for every boy hero. She is lovely and just dumb enough … but beware of those happily-ever-afters! They are a snare and a delusion. Princesses, no matter how beguiling, have their price and the rest of the story is indeed unwritten.

Materials for making the Usual Princess:

1/4 yd for dress (skirt, bodice and sleeves and sleeve linings)
1/4 yd for cape
1/4 yd for petticoat
Scrap of felt for shoes and crown
1/2 yd ribbon for cape
Loose goat hair, dyed if necessary

Body

1 Trace the appliqué patterns for dress. Take note of the arrow, which will tell you where the appliqué pattern begins and ends.

2 Cut the pieces for the body and appliqués for the dress from selected fabric. Stack the appliqué on the body, which is the base fabric, and stay stitch it in place. Cover the raw edges that will not be caught in the seam with a satin zigzag stitch.

3 Put the two body pieces with right sides together. Place some poly-fil at the side of the nose next to the stitch plate so that it will flip into the seam. Stitch the body, leaving open where indicated on the pattern piece. Clip, turn, and stuff firmly. Close, by hand, using a ladder stitch.

4 Cut the breast from the dress fabric. Dart them as you did for Mother. Trim off the excess fabric and gather with matching quilting thread. Leave an opening the size of a dime at the back of the breast and stuff firmly. She is oh, so very perky. Press them to the body and stitch in place with the ladder stitch.

Arms and Legs

1 The fabric for the leg and arms will be the selected flesh colored fabric. Cut pattern pieces.

2 With right sides together, stitch the legs and the arms, leave open on leg where indicated to turn. Make a tiny slash (1/2"),

through one layer of the arm to turn. Clip, turn, and stuff firmly. Close by hand.

Find the directions for sculpting the face, hands, and feet on pages 60-63.

Find the instructions about painting the mothers face on page 61.

Skirt

1 Cut the skirt 8" x 22-1/2". The petticoat is 9" x 22-1/2". Fold both of them width-wise, with right sides together and stitch, leaving an opening at the top of each one of 1-1/2" to slip them onto the doll. Press the seam, and top stitch the opening for both. Press a rolled hem at the bottom of the skirt and petticoat and stitch in place.

2 Two layers of 22-1/2" is a lot of bulk to fit around that doll so gather by hand with a knotted thread. Pull the gathers to fit around her waist. Make it fit a little on the high side as she is ever so demure. Tie off the thread and stay stitch the gathers in place.

3 Cut the waistband 1-1/2" x 7-1/2". Fit the right side of the waistband to the wrong side of the waist of the skirt. Center to center. Pin. There should be overlap. Wrap the ends of the band 3/8" to finish the ends. Stitch in place.

4 Turn the ends of the band. Press. Fold under a tiny hem at the raw edge and with wrong sides together top stitch the band at the front of the skirt. Now place it on her and hand-tack it in place.

5 Sleeves – now pay attention and see if you can figure this out. Cut out four sleeves for the lining and four for the jacket. Stitch the sleeves in pairs with right sides together, matching sleeves with sleeves and lining with lining.

6 Press the seams open. With right sides together, stitch the pairs of lining to the pairs of the jacket on the flat side. Press.

7 Fold each unit lengthwise and, with right sides together, stitch around the outer edge. Leave an opening on the lining to turn.

Turn and stuff the lining into the sleeve. Put the sleeve on top of the arm before attaching the arm to the body.

See page 64 for instructions on how to assemble the body.

Cape

1 Cut out the cape and lining from selected fabric.

2 With right sides together, stitch the cape to the lining. Leave open at the neck. Turn and press. Turn the raw edge in and cover it with the 1/2 yd of ribbon. Center to center. Tie the cape in place.

Shoes

1 Cut the shoes from felt scraps. Stitch where indicated on the pattern piece.

2 Press the two seams together and stitch a point. Start the arc at the point indicated on the pattern piece. Turn and slip over her none too dainty feet. Close around her lovely ankle with a button.

Crown and Hair

1 Stitch the tufts of blond loose goat hair (aren't Princesses always blond?) about the head of the princess for the desired effect. Tie off with a colonial knot.

2 Cut the crown from a scrap of felt. Make a circle of it and stitch the two short ends together. Turn.

3 Plop that crown on her head at angle. Perhaps a little confetti would be in order as just another Usual Princess is sacrificed for Jack.

The Hen and the Golden Eggs

h, we have come to the hen, her cleverly painted Eggs (which look a lot like beans), and so it goes around. The solution lies very close to the magic. I think of prayer that way, close to the source. As an artist, I have found that my connection to the infinite, by way of thanksgiving, praise, and inspiration, is life-giving, just like those Golden Eggs. And it is portable. I believe that what I do is a form of praise to the giver of all good gifts. What strikes me here in the story is that the Giant *hoards* the eggs from his golden hen. He counts them and puts them in bags. Jack takes the hen and gives it to his mother like the good son that he is. What do we do with our gifts, our inspirations? Do we protect them, squirrel them away, clutch, and grab for fear that they will vanish? As the poet Kahlil Gibran said:

"For what are your possessions but things you keep and guard for fear you may need them tomorrow? And tomorrow, what shall tomorrow bring to the over prudent dog burying bones in the trackless and as he follows the Pilgrims to the holy city? And what is fear of need but need itself? Is not the dread of thirst when your well is Full, the thirst that is unquenchable?"

It has been my experience that giving simply makes a place for receiving, and I have never found it to fail. Nothing really belongs to us anyway except our freedom of choice; choosing to be a creative conduit allows us to share, to magnify. The Hen I offer is made like a Japanese purse, with the addition of a fabric feather or two for effect, and is simple enough to warrant your giving a few away, along with a Golden Egg or two.

Materials for making the Hen:

Scrap of woven cotton for the Hen and her wings

2-1/4 yd pieces of woven cotton for the two fringed feathers

Pearl cotton and two star shaped buttons for the feet and the legs of the chicken

Seed beads, beads slightly larger and sequins for the Hen's comb and eye

Scrap of rickrack for wings

Instructions for Making the Hen

1 Cut the Hen's body, wings and wing lining from selected fabric. With right sides together, stitch each wing with its lining together. Leave open where indicated on the pattern piece. Turn and press. Stitch rickrack on the curved side. Turn under the edge on rickrack to stop fraying.

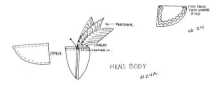

2 With right sides together, stitch the Hen's body. Leave open where indicated on the pattern piece. Turn and stuff. Pin the two seams together to hold in stuffing. The feathers will go in this opening.

3 To create the tail feathers, cut out four layers of selected fab-

rics for each. Fold the feathers where indicated on the paper pattern. Stitch on that fold. Starting at the large end or base of the feather, clip as indicated to create rag feathers. Mount into the open end of the Hen. Stitch her closed with the two seams pressed together and the raw edges folded in.

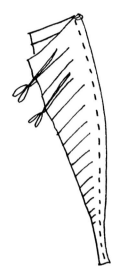

4 Mount the wings on the Hen by hand where indicated. Make a pocket out of one so she can hold some of her golden eggs. Unorthodox, but convenient.

5 Use a fine-tipped permanent marking pen to draw in the beak. Color it red with a brush-tipped fabric pen.

6 Thread your needle with pearl cotton – no knot. Enter the Hen at the tale and bring the needle to the bottom seam where the legs might be. Form a colonial knot. The pearl cotton legs will be 2-1/2" long. String on a star button from the bottom of the button, re-enter the remaining hole. Allow for the 2-1/2" leg and re-enter the body a few threads

from where you exited. Take a tiny stitch to anchor. Repeat for the remaining leg and foot and tie off the leg with a colonial knot at the body of the Hen.

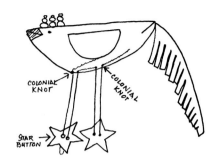

7 To make a comb for the Hen (well, she has one), use a beading needle and nylon beading thread. Form a colonial knot on the head of the Hen. String the slightly larger bead first and then the seed bead. Bring the needle through the larger bead, using the seed bead as a stopper. Enter the head again and exit next the first stack of beads. String another large bead, then a seed bead, re-enter the large bead and re-enter the head. Repeat one more time. Tie off the process with a colonial knot.

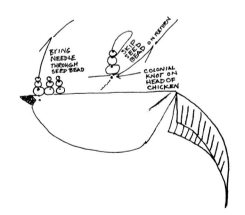

8 For the eye, repeat what you did for the comb but use the sequin instead of the larger bead.

The Rest of the Story

Lastly, we have this thoroughly co-dependent Harp. She seems to be very connected to the Giant in a most unhealthy way. "Sing!" demands the Giant. Her music is lovely and Jack steals her away as she cries out to her master. Don't we all carry within us a connection to the problem that keeps us from solving it? Something that we are not clearly in charge of, that sings in a compelling way and often acts against us? Isn't there a part of us that is so uncomfortable with change that it would prefer misery rather than deal with the unknown? Ah, yes, well stealing that and taking charge of it may be the only way to set yourself free – both personally and artistically. Now I must tell you the harp was delightful to make and I spent more time on her than I did on the others. There's no explaining that, right?

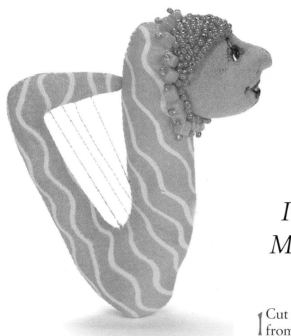

Materials for making the Harp:

Scraps of fabric to make the harp and the face
Gold hand embroidery floss
Beading needle, beading thread and beads and seed beads to go around the head
Button, Carpet, and Craft thread

Instructions for Making the Harp

1 Cut out the Harp and the face from selected fabric.

2 With right sides together, stitch the Harp. Leave open where indicated on the pattern piece. Clip, turn, and stuff firmly. Close the opening by hand.

3 With right sides together, stitch the face with a bit of poly-fil at the nose. Leave open at the back. Clip and turn

4 Gather around the face using the #7 long darner and the Button, Carpet and Craft needle. Knot the thread. Pull the gathers until you could fit a dime in the opening. Tie off the thread with a colonial knot. Stuff firmly and ladder stitch in place over the opening in the Harp.

Refer to page 60-61 to sculpt the face and paint it.

5 Stack a medium bead and a seed bead around the head as described for the Hen on page 78. Stitch on one bead at a time to form a peak at the top of the head. String the bead on the beading needle and secure it in place by stitching into head and picking up another bead.

6 Make the strings on the harp using the #7 long darner and metallic gold thread. Enter the Harp at the side and exit at #1. Form a colonial knot. Stitch down the harp to form the strings as shown in the illustration below. Tie off with another colonial knot. Lovely. Enjoy the music.

The End

The doll form has taken me many places, both in my head and in my body. Along the way, I have found companions who have given context to my vision and informed my dreams. Noreen and I met, not at the beginning and certainly not at the end, but in the middle where there exists enough delightful confusion, banners, and streamers for a good romp. Thanks to the magic hands, editors, camera wizards, and publishers who watched and took note while we played!